Coaching for Cultural Transformation

Coaching for Cultural Transformation

Staying competitive in shifting environments

John Cockburn-Evans

 Open University Press

Open University Press
McGraw Hill
8th Floor, 338 Euston Road
London
England
NW1 3BH

email: enquiries@openup.co.uk
world wide web: www.openup.co.uk

First edition published 2021

A catalogue record of this book is available from the British Library

ISBN-13: 9780335249275
ISBN-10: 0335249272
eISBN: 9780335249282

Library of Congress Cataloging-in-Publication Data
CIP data applied for

Typeset by Transforma Pvt. Ltd., Chennai, India

Praise for this book

"This book is timeless, undeniably practical, refreshingly realistic, and 100% on point. Generous and humble from beginning to end, John provides an indispensable primer and guide in key culture and coaching models, frameworks, and assessments, as well as the distinctions between individual, group and team coaching, all presented in an easy-to-read style.

Readers will find his counsel on hostile cultures, understanding resistance, coaching teams and groups, and taking the personal risk to speak up particularly rich in truth and sustenance.

Every leader and coach embarking on a culture change or transformation programme should read this first and keep it close to hand throughout the journey!"

—Sehaam Cyrene PCC, Founder, Better Conversations & Associates

"This book provides a great overview for any business considering using coaching as part of a change programme. Coaches and Management Consultants would also be able to use the models, which are clearly explained."

—Jacqui Elmore, Business Coach, Ology Coaching

"This is a very insightful and thought-provoking book. I've known John for ten years and quickly learned that he is a consummate chemical engineer, lean practitioner, guide, and coach. This work captures a wealth of his expertise in the latter areas. John takes what could be dry concepts and injects colour by relating his own personal experiences to each topic being explained."

—Peter L. King, Founder and President, Lean Dynamics LLC

"Corporate culture underpins competitive advantage. Achieving cultural transformation requires a delicate balance of emotions, logic and experience. John brilliantly blends these together with his engineering background and consulting and coaching expertise. He delivers rigorous coaching principles through a practitioner's view to bridge the gap between forecasts and results."

—Hugh Page, Managing Director, Integrated Value Consulting

"John has cracked the code of successful cultural transformation. His book is a primer that lays out the most business effective roadmap to guide sustainable change."

—James B. Porter, Jr., Former Vice President,
E. I. DuPont and Company

"People thrive at the heart of every successful business – John Cockburn-Evans drives directly at this incredibly important subject in this great read, providing clarity and insight alongside accessible common sense logic. This book is a must-read for anyone considering or involved in a cultural change programme."

—Daemmon Reeve, CEO Treatt PLC

"John Cockburn-Evans presents a refreshingly candid reflection on his own experiences as both a management consultant and a certified business coach. As the author himself acknowledges this is not a how-to manual but a theoretically informed discussion of John's vast cache of first-hand industry knowledge. To this end, the narrative is punctuated with autobiographical vignettes, all of which bring a sense of empirical colour and vital qualification to the specific arguments advanced. This all makes for a genuinely accessible pedagogical resource."

—Tom Vine, Associate Professor, Suffolk
Business School

"John has encapsulated his vast experience into a comprehensive overview of this fascinating subject. It is an incredibly useful reference for both the experienced practitioner and for the interested individual. Personally, I have already used it as a reference point, to consider how to approach specific issues whilst coaching colleagues."

—Ian White, Managing Director, Beckett Investment
Management Group Ltd.

"This book is a must-read primer for coaches and business leaders who recognise that cultural transformation is key to competitive advantage. John has written a practical guide on using multi-level organisational coaching to manage and embed business critical change, combining useful concepts and models with practical examples that can be put into practice right away. Read this book and learn from John's experience and success."

—Georgina Woudstra, MCC, Founder & Principal,
Team Coaching Studio

Contents

List of figures and tables

Figures

Table

Preface

The book contains examples based on my experience as a coach, with reference to generally accepted theories. I have tried to inject some humour to reinforce my points, with specific takeaways at the end of each chapter. The aim of this book is to connect some conceptual thinking with some personal examples and experiences of coaching while working through cultural transformation. Hopefully, it will provide some context and perspective as a guide, rather than be a 'How to Coach' manual. It should also provide some guidance for leaders and influencers on the impact coaching can have in a change project or transformation, and guide when and how to use coaching effectively. The reader will see recurring themes and some level of repetition, which is deliberate to embed the learning.

Throughout the book I have made reference to professional coaches; these are coaches who not only have experience, but also are professionally trained, hold the relevant qualifications and abide by a code of ethics that is generally common across professional bodies, such as the International Coach Federation (ICF), the Academy of Executive Coaching (AoEC) and other organisations. The word coaching is a very generic term with many meanings encompassing numerous coaches with varying experience, training, abilities and certification. 'Coaching' does not require a certificate to practise at present, which means not all coaches are held to the same professional standards. That does not mean that such coaches cannot add value, certainly on large projects. As a rule, I will always select coaches with relevant training and qualifications, but some internal coaches are selected as large clients want to develop their people. At this point I suggest to the client they gain certification, and during their development I ask that these coaches abide by the core principles of coaching and ethics, particularly with respect to confidentiality.

I will refer to previous operational experiences and consulting engagements, but clients' names, and individuals' names and locations have been changed for reasons of confidentiality.

About the author

I started my working life as a chartered chemical engineer, accomplished operational leader and transformational expert. I have worked extensively in the petrochemical and manufacturing industries in the areas of operational excellence, construction, and engineering management. My career history has included working initially for the chemical giant BASF, then Total and, latterly, DuPont. After 25 years in operations, I moved into management consultancy.

I moved on to an area of work which became one of my passions in the early 2000s: 'Lean Management' and productivity. Having delivered successful lean projects and supporting the European site transformation teams on their lean journey, I decided to make the move into management consultancy, which had been another of my interests. I wanted to share my desire and experiences. I also had a hankering to become a business coach and after my initial coach training as a neuro-linguistic programming (NLP) practitioner in 2008, I followed up with a formal coaching diploma in 2014, becoming qualified as an ICF coach at PCC level in 2018.

In 2010, I joined the DuPont consulting arm, where I embarked on a major operational excellence transformation project for the largest petrochemical company in Russia, as a senior consultant. This was followed by various other consulting assignments in Eastern Europe, as a principal, in heavy industries such as steel, where I was able to put my coaching skills, operational excellence and project management skills to good use, culminating in acting as market leader. I now run my own consultancy, working for a variety of large and small clients in the UK, Europe, Eastern Europe and the Middle East, specifically working with cultural transformation, project execution and productivity. In addition, I work as an independent leadership coach, business ambassador for the Institute of Directors, East of England. I have given several talks and short lectures for business organisations, and have designed and delivered an MBA module on Change Management. As a Fellow of the Institution of Chemical Engineers, I mentor young graduates towards their chartered status in addition to mentoring start-up companies.

Acknowledgements

First and foremost, I would like to thank all those who encouraged me through my formative years in the corporate world and especially my father who pushed me to pursue my then passion of engineering, rather than follow him into the legal profession. He unfortunately died in 2010 at the start of my first consulting assignment in Russia, so I never got to tell him that I had been 'sent to Siberia'.

I would also like to acknowledge all my coaching peers and associates who have helped me on my coaching journey so far. Specifically, I would like to thank Sue Bayliss, Master NLP Practitioner, who awakened me to coaching and my non-technical skills, and Rosi Torriani, who encouraged me to follow coaching more formally while consulting at DuPont. I would like to acknowledge my more recent associates and good friends who have pushed me deeper and harder into coaching, and particularly Sehaam Cyrene, who kept me honest writing this book.

Acknowledgements

1   Introduction

Overview

Why did I embark on this book? I must say that as a child and with a technical appreciation, I was not exactly impassioned by prose and writing and actively used to avoid it. Numbers and equations were more my thing. It was relatively late in my career that I started to enjoy this aspect of work. There were a couple of specific points in time that when I reflect, I noticed a change in myself. These were to be the trigger points that led me out of operations and into consultancy. First, as a DuPont leader, I was fortunate to go on some great training courses and leadership events. I remember, circa 2003, I was at the end of a two-week intensive leadership development course run by the Institute of Management Development in Lausanne, and I had my initial exposure to the concepts and workings of Myers–Briggs[1] when I first realised that I had potentially some other softer skills that I had not explored. Although the existence of the so-called 'left' and 'right' brains is now being challenged by behavioural psychologists, they are useful labels to elucidate the differences between the processing and emotional aspects of the brain function. Generally, it is accepted that the right side of the brain controls the creative aspects, and the left the processing function. My results showed me right in the middle of both, and moreover I did not stray too far from the centre in each direction. Oddly enough, I am left-handed. This hit me like the proverbial train. I had been interested in science, equations processing and logic all my life. Furthermore, I was a practising engineer who spent his life planning and using Gantt charts. This was the first seed of the alternative perspective on myself.

Second, I vividly recall my first formal coach training with Sue Bayliss where we covered concepts of being 'In Time' vs. being driven by in a mode, that is 'Through Time'.[2] People who are In Time spend more time enjoying the moment, and those in Through Time spend more time reflecting on the past, and planning the future. Generally, the former is associated more with Eastern cultures and the latter with Western cultures. I had expected that I would be more Through Time, given my technical background. However, going through some of Sue's exercises, and getting more independent feedback, it was clear that I was more In Time. As I reflected on this, it made more and more sense. In my younger days I had enjoyed skiing and being in 'flow'. I also had a penchant for fast cars, which later led me to amateur racing. This state challenged my original thinking, in a way that made me consider myself as more creative and was the trigger for my future role in consulting. On reflection, I realised that I had created my own technically based paradigm in my formative years and early career. Why do I mention this particularly? Because as coaches we learn to be non-judgemental, and must avoid putting ideas, concepts and people into enclosed spaces or little boxes.

As I went through my personal discovery process, I asked myself a series of questions:

- Why was context so important to me at the initiation of any project or key activity?
- Why did I enjoy the personal interactions as much as the actual physical work in any project?
- Why had I always felt like a frustrated salesman?
- Why was I a good negotiator?
- Why did I feel more comfortable in the company of women at work, and enjoy working on projects with them?
- Why did I enjoy being challenged, and having the 'freedom to operate'?

Answering all these questions helped me move forward on the journey. I remember clearly doing a fun exercise at our client's in Siberia, where our leader and vice president asked us, out of interest, how many of us were left-handed. Of the 20 there at that time, more than 15 were left-handed. Only 10–15 per cent of the population is left-handed. There is a belief that left-handers have more maverick tendencies. This was not a scientific study, but it might explain why a large proportion were working in corporate consultancy with all its idiosyncrasies and pressures. In her HuffPost article, 'How left-handed people think and feel differently: being a leftie is far from a disadvantage', Carolyn Gregoire describes some of the advantages of being left-handed, based on research, and states it is not considered an evolutionary weakness.[3]

Building on the previous points, I found out very quickly that the best consulting pitches I ever delivered were those that were co-delivered with a female colleague. It might not be considered egalitarian or appropriate, and maybe even manipulative to actively seek a gender balanced sales pitch team, but it works. I believe that this is driven by the fact that potential clients see the balance and find it more difficult to find fault. I have subsequently spoken to both male and female coaches and consultants and they have experienced the same.

Not a coaching manual

As we progress through this book, hopefully this thread will become clear. I decided to write on this topic for many reasons. First, considerable numbers of books have already been dedicated to the subject of change management and cultural transformation.

There are well-understood and practised models for change, such as the 8-step model from John Kotter[4] and others. There are fewer books on cultural transformation, and few of these that link the power of coaching to cultural transformation or effective change management. The only one I came across was *Coaching for Change*[5] by John L. Bennet and Mary Wayne Bush, which covers such topics as the coaching process, leadership requirements in organisations and wider issues such as cross-cultural boundaries. I will also touch on these issues, but this book will not be a 'how to coach manual'. My experience in consultancy as a transformational leader has shown me the power of formal coaching. We all coach informally daily, as part of our working inter-actions, usually in short bursts as we guide people through their work, whether it is a short session on the shop floor, or at the end of a meeting. The word coaching can be considered nebulous and a catch-all for any interaction that guides or facilitates a person or situation. Therefore, I distinguish between formal and informal coaching. In this sense, formal coaching means coaching as part of an agreed programme with strategic and specific outcomes in mind. The cadence and duration of the programme will be determined by the change programme sponsors, with expert guidance from coaches and coach leaders[6] as a way of achieving the desired outcomes. Formal coaching not only facilitates the outcomes, but it holds leaders accountable for regular interaction with change agents and key stakeholders. Far too often, leaders charge ahead with activities, and even if there are formal communication programmes in place, coaching gives time for people to reflect and breathe. Apart from creative agen-cies,[7] such as branding, marketing and advertising, most of the larger traditional com-panies are selling a technical or tangible product. This historically has required their employees to have a strong technical or scientific education. Their education is their bedrock, which means that they are generally process-driven, with potentially less room for engagement with their emotions. Quality coaching gives the staff the oppor-tunity to engage in deeper thought and make a better connection with their emotions.

These reasons for coaching may seem soft, but I will demonstrate that there are clear definite benefits in support of a change programme, and moreover that a coaching culture will lead to more sustainable change, and significantly improve the chances of delivering faster and more effective future change programmes.

There are a multitude of coaching models and approaches, and I will reference one or two of them. It is not the intent of this book to compare these models in terms of value or impact, but to illustrate how effective coaching programmes can sup-port significant change within organisations, if executed properly. In my experi-ence, coaching alone will not bring about significant organisational and sustainable change. It is just one element and should be done in conjunction with training and systemic process change. There are numerous coaching approaches that come under the auspices of neuro-linguistic programming, for instance, in addition to suites of other approaches I have been taught. When coaching individuals, I select the approach that best fits their needs and the sustainable outcomes they desire. Coaching is truly a process of facilitation. I avoid using the term 'tools', which I have heard used elsewhere. The word tool can imply a 'fixing' process. This will not support an effective coaching process, because nobody really wants to be 'fixed'.

2 Problem statement: Discuss the general challenges for effective cultural transformation, state why some fail, and why some are successful

Context and VUCA

As always, the best place to start is with the challenge. Organisations are continually being challenged to perform better in terms of sales, profit, cost reduction, growth, etc. This is more prevalent currently than ever before. The often used term VUCA (volatile, uncertain, complex, ambiguous) describes the current working environment for business, implying it is fast-moving and variable, making it less predictable. The concept was devised by the American military to help understand difficult and challenging battle scenarios. Globalisation, increased competition, advancing technology are all putting greater stress on organisations. Each aspect will create stress for businesses on its own, but in combination, the total stress will also create another level of confusion. Companies need to understand the marketplace and have the agility to deal with the changing conditions, this is now the business imperative.

Technology is moving at an exponential pace. As an example, a processor doubles in capacity every two years. Furthermore, the amount of data space within a PC will double every two years, and battery capacity required for a fixed computing load will halve every two years. The former fact has been true since 1990 and the latter since 1945.[1]

Technology is only one challenge, but with robotics and artificial intelligence (AI), then the manufacturing space required for a given output is reducing. There is a huge associated opportunity for cost reduction, but if you have committed to purchasing buildings, long leases or fixed data centres, that creates a challenge. The organisation must be agile to stay ahead. This is inexorably linked to the 'uncertainty' element of VUCA. If we now look at 'volatility', we must factor in globalisation and geopolitics, which are currently in a heightened state of alert. The looming trade war between the USA and China is a clear example. Furthermore, certain economies are booming, some are shrinking. The rate of change is a lot shorter than 10 years ago. The advent of crypto currencies is also a factor. These are traded online and continuously, with high and low market positions switching quickly. The level of complexity has increased driven by technology, computing power and the use of simple algorithms to make decisions. Machines can be monitored and maintained remotely, requiring different skill sets for maintenance staff, and rendering certain types of mechanic obsolete. There has always been a level of 'ambiguity' in business, but this is being compounded by the other three uncomfortable elements. This is creating a cocktail of confusion for business leaders and making it more difficult to have a clear strategy.

Initial approach

As a means of aiding understanding, and for greater simplicity, I will refer in this book to the four 'Ws' and the one 'H', i.e. Why, What, Where, When and How. My preamble has covered the Why. The four Ws and one H have great relevance in two ways. First, in any change management or cultural transformation journey, these are exactly the questions that leaders should be asking before they embark. We will see the close relation between these, and the structure of the change management models in Chapter 5. Second, these are exactly the questions coaches should be pondering as a means of preparation before any coaching session with an individual or team. The 'Why' in particular and the others will flow during the sessions. Of course, in the case of the 'How', this is what the team or individuals should be working on themselves, rather than being told or instructed.

Continuous improvement

Businesses must continually review and update their strategies and create a culture of agility. Some would argue that not all companies must be agile to grow and survive. Some products and markets stay stable with minimal development, the classic and retro car market being one. For large corporations to be agile takes considerable effort. To be truly agile, the culture needs to be prevalent from top to bottom. In any organisation, the 'engine room' is driven by the first-line supervisors and their equivalents. From my consulting experience, sustainable change only ever happens if every level in the organisation is 'touched'. Leaders need to understand they have to 'let go' and they can increase their personal bandwidth by pushing as much work practically down the pyramid on the basis the personnel are adequately

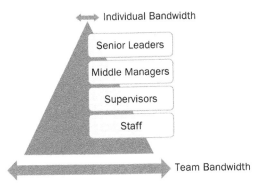

Figure 2.1 Staff bandwidth pyramid

trained, and there are quality assurance processes in place (Figure 2.1). This will include both knowledge transfer and coaching.

The above summarises the 'How', but let's look at the 'What'. I will aim to cover what is required of a successful culture, and provide some examples of a poor one. There is a certain level of paradox in cultural change or transformation, in that a culture that is going to change may not be best placed to effect the change required.

Let us look at the characteristics of some cultures of organisations that will not be supportive of 'change'. I will look at these characteristics in more depth when we review change models.

Drivers, challenges and energy

First of all, any organisation needs to have the drive, energy and passion for change. Without these characteristics, an organisation is going nowhere. This must come from the top and filter down. This also relates to the pyramid. Some larger organisations do not have this level of vibrancy and internal politics can stifle any passion. Most managers and employees have the best of intentions, but the energy becomes lost. I recall working in a smaller company where the leaders were very passionate about the business because it was a family business; what they failed to recognise was that they were passionate, because they were all making good money, but the lower echelons were not. It is difficult to feel passionate about a business when you are not seeing the benefits. If a company is truly going to effect a cultural transformation, all levels of the organisation must feel passionate.

Organisational cultures, by their very nature, are embedded. Immature company cultures[2] will be heavily influenced either by the owner, the board or the culture of the region. Geert Hofstede[3] has done considerable work on interculturality, and provides models supported by data to compare different cultures in six different dimensions. What is culture? 'Culture can be defined as the ideas, customs and social behavior of a particular people or society and/or the collective programming of the mind that distinguishes members of one category of people from others.'[4] Put simply, a culture is what shapes the social rules, framework and norms of a region, country or company. The interrelation between a wider regional culture, the corporate culture and even a site culture can be interesting. In my experience, a culture can flow in many directions. A regional culture can influence a site culture and a corporate culture should be influencing a site culture, assuming the corporate culture is appropriate. According to Michael Barrier:

> Corporate culture refers to the shared values, attitudes, standards, and beliefs that characterize members of an organization and define its nature. Corporate culture is rooted in an organization's goals, strategies, structure, and approaches to labor, customers, investors, and the greater community. As such, it is an essential component in any business's ultimate success or failure.[5]

In my world, a corporate culture is what defines it in terms of its vision, values and processes, and the way it goes about its business. One of the keys to the success of any change programme implementation is understanding the company culture and its influence on its staff, and how it is influenced itself by wider aspects of culture.

As I mentioned earlier, company culture will initially be heavily influenced by other external factors. This means that it is not easy to move. 'Culture eats strategy for lunch'[6] is a well-known expression. The message is clear: as culture is strong and embedded, it will consume other efforts such as strategy, unless there is a proper programme to shift it. This will be covered later in the book.

There is another challenge: humans like routine and fear change, so sticking with the status quo is more comfortable. Even the most enlightened members of the organisation can resist change. Change requires energy and effort. This links to the point earlier around passion – passion requires a level of energy and our energy as human beings is finite.

The next point also links to the above; any change requires a level of open-mindedness, and the ability to listen, take in the proposed changes and understand the rationale behind them. Open-mindedness is talked about considerably these days, and there are trainings and coaching techniques to improve it. A lot of people consider that they are open-minded, but levels of open-mindedness are linked to personal levels of self-awareness. The iceberg model[7] is a great way of illustrating how culture can be impacted by an individual's beliefs and values (Figure 2.2).

We generally see the top half of the iceberg, which is the behaviours, i.e. the visible manifestation. We do not initially see below the waterline, which are the values and beliefs, which have been nurtured for years and have a huge impact on how we perceive what is above in the world. Another way of looking at it is as the conscious world that sits above the subconscious world. It is very difficult to shift values and beliefs, but they can be moulded to a new corporate culture with the correct approach.

Another element that has a loose connection with the open-mindedness is not having a fear of the future, which is not the same as fear of change. Fear of the future is more linked to the lack of certainty, and some people need certainty as a bedrock. I have run numerous career orientation exercises with people over the years.[8] The simple questionnaire covers five career orientations or dimensions,

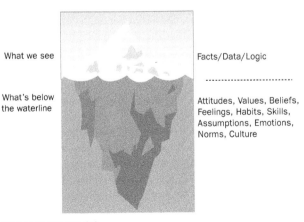

What we see — Facts/Data/Logic

What's below the waterline — Attitudes, Values, Beliefs, Feelings, Habits, Skills, Assumptions, Emotions, Norms, Culture

Figure 2.2 The iceberg model

which are defined as 'Getting Ahead', Getting Challenged', 'Getting Free', 'Getting Balanced' and 'Getting Secure'. The latter is about job security, and in uncertain times, this may be connected to a fear of the future. Although this is slightly off topic, it is amazing how enlightening this approach is. Many a time, I have seen folks with unrealistic goals, but who have not had the foresight to challenge themselves. Typical examples are people in their late forties in a lower middle management position within a large corporation but who see themselves as the next CEO. This process is amazingly enlightening for them, and quite often sets them free from their own self-generated and metaphorical shackles.

Some organisations are just very poor at execution. Any shift in culture requires a system as well as creativity and thinking to change it. We are not talking about a complex system, but a framework and measure that will push people to the end goal. Some organisations are very transactional; this can help with delivery and execution, but can also stifle creative thinking. Other organisations are very collegiate in nature, with a lot of sharing and consequent discussion. It will be a question of getting the balance right and holding people accountable. Ensuring accountability in large organisations will be difficult, due to the complexity of the management chain. A simple cascade process, where each level holds itself accountable for its own results and outcomes, and the level below responsible for action, always works. I am always amazed how even well-established and sophisticated organisations do not understand simple RACI diagrams.[9] Again, I will cover the importance of accountability and how it can be coached as a separate specific topic.

I have briefly mentioned execution, but I would now like to turn to planning. As we would imagine, some organisations are better at planning than others. It is imperative that there is a strong plan but also a realistic plan for cultural change or transformation. There are two ends of the spectrum. Some plans are way too detailed for the strategic intent of the change and some are not detailed enough. In any cultural transformation, it is important to get early traction. This means having a plan that does not delay or bog itself down, or confuse the staff involved with it. The appropriate level of detail is important. Quite often leaders think that because they have the vision, they have all the details at the start. This is a mistake, as cultural change is a journey, which means it will be impossible to have all the details of the plan at the start. In other cases, there is not enough detail in the plan to execute it effectively. This usually means that the milestones are unclear and contain too many intangibles. The final element of any plan is that it must be realistic – in terms of both timing and content. In this sense, content refers to all the elements that are required to execute the plan in terms of money, resources and activity details. The timing element is critical. In my experience, these plans are usually unrealistic as they lack the required detail to be executed.

At the time of writing, I am on a consulting engagement for a major cultural transformation for a petrochemicals company. I am coaching on the mindsets and behaviours (metanoia) of key staff, but unfortunately they have had an unexpected critical event which is heavily impacting on the business. I have had to drop out of the planned coaching programme for a while and help them to get back on their feet on a manufacturing unit, with guidance on rapid project execution. As always, the client falls into a familiar trap by setting unrealistic timing due to business pressure, i.e. start-up date is fixed immediately without any regard to the activities required, the sequencing and any details of the tasks. An unexpected shutdown or major deviation means that not all the data was available, formatted correctly or analysed appropriately, i.e. work must be done on it. As the remediation plan is developed, the pressure on staff ratchets up as business leaders demand answers. This is what I call 'rushing to fail', where ill thought-out answers are often shared with the leaders. What is required is time to think, and logical sequencing as the data is gathered. Experienced and educated planners are required to collate the data and sequence it. Undue pressure will lead to poor planning and shortcuts, which will not speed things up, but will cause delays and recycles, as the real situation starts to become obvious. This is the situation I am in right now, where I am consulting with knowledge and experience on the theory and coaching the key stakeholders to think and behave differently. I am also supporting the planners and experts with coaching to help them stand up and demonstrate their expertise. I am always amazed how many experts are hired and then ignored when things do not go to plan. I recall in the early 1990s, when Toyota was building its factory in Derbyshire, seeing a sign at the side of the A38, 'Land acquired for Toyota'. I was commuting every weekend to a new job in the Midlands, and the sign seemed to be there for ages, and then the factory appeared, almost miraculously. This is the mastery of the Japanese culture and detailed planning. Nothing happens in construction until all the required detail is in place. Failure to plan properly causes inefficiency, delays and recycles. I have been unfortunately in many construction jobs, where the pressure to see bricks and mortar earlier than was required has led to project delays. This is just one example of getting planning right; the same theory applies to business planning, and I will come back to this later. Toyota's Burnaston factory opened in 1992 and was a great example of rapid and effective construction.

I will come to vision in more detail in later chapters where I discuss transformational models, as having an appropriate vision for the change is essential. However, for the moment, I would like to touch on aligning the vision to the plan, assuming you have both. Quite often the visioning process for any change is harder than expected, and then getting a plan to support the vision will probably be more difficult. This is where I will go into more detail on alignment and how coaching can really have an impact. Having proper alignment of people, systems and all the elements of a change or cultural programme is essential and there will be many touchpoints on the journey. Furthermore, at the end of a visioning process, the outcomes often are clear only to those who have been responsible for generating the vision, not those who are affected. This presents another considerable challenge. This is another area where coaching will have a huge impact.

Thinking of structure and roles

As we start to consider the additional elements of any cultural journey, let us think about accountability. It may be obvious but there must be clear accountability for any cultural change programme from the board, to senior leaders and to those who have been asked to execute the change programme. In my experience, having clear

	Business Idea	Concept	Project Plan	Design	Fabrication	Installation	Commissioning
Business Owner	A/R	R	C	C	I	I	I
Head Designer	C	A	C	A	C	I	I
Designer	I	C	I	R	C	I	C
Project Manager	I	I	A	C	A	A	A
Planner		I	R	I	I	I	I
Fabricator			C	I	R	r	I
Installation Eng.			I	I	I	R	C
Field Engineer						I	R

Figure 2.3 A typical RACI chart

accountability chains in any programme is essential and is often skimmed over or almost forgotten. You can guarantee if there are no clear accountabilities and the programme goes off track, then the 'blame game' will start. One of the contributory factors is that not everyone can truly identify the difference between accountability and responsibility. In some languages there is no difference. This can create considerable confusion. While on my first large consulting engagement in Russia, I learned that this was the case. We were struggling with getting people on the client side to take accountability for driving the changes required of the operational excellence programme we had designed. We were getting confused and frustrated. One of our Russian analysts explained the challenge to us. In Russia, if you are held accountable, you are responsible too. As you can imagine, this creates an enormous challenge for effective delegation. There is an expectation that if you are accountable, you are going to deliver the work yourself. This is a huge opportunity for inefficiencies. There are other cultural dynamics such as hierarchy and power distance[10] in the Russian culture that come into play. It is fair to say that a large swathe of politicians struggle with the concept of accountability. Accountability is generally singular and thus deeply personal. It is driven by our values and beliefs, which are moulded in our formative years by our family, our experiences and the regional or country culture. One of the tools often used in project execution is the RACI chart (Figure 2.3). A RACI chart details who is *R*esponsible, who is *A*ccountable, who needs to be *C*onsulted and who needs to be *I*nformed for any group of activities. Figure 2.3 is a simple illustrative RACI chart (a manufacturing example is given for clarity). Examples for a cultural transformation programme can easily be generated.

You can see from Figure 2.3 that it provides clarity on roles. It is possible for senior people to have multiple accountabilities, in this case the project manager who is accountable for the delivery of the whole project. However, activities should generally not have more than one owner or accountable person as confusion will ensue in execution challenges. There are very few cases where work activities or work elements are joint accountabilities. These tend to be where there is a clear legal framework, such as for a board of directors. You will also notice in this example that we have A/R in the case of the business owner. This is because they were accountable for the validity of the initial concept or business idea, but also responsible for developing it to a point where the head designer could do something meaningful with it. To round off the example, you will also see the use of 'r'. This can happen in a few instances, where there is a primary responsibility for one activity and a secondary responsibility for another related activity. In this case, the fabricator has primary responsibility for fabricating the product and a secondary responsibility for helping to install it, supported with tacit knowledge. I will come back to the effective use of RACI diagrams in the context of cultural transformation supported by coaching in the context of the team coaching environment.

Thinking of team selection

I am going to move on to the challenges of team selection. If you are going to make significant organisational changes and effect a transformation process, then as one would expect you need to have the correct team. Creating the right team means getting the people not only with the correct functional skills, but also with the correct emotional capabilities. The concept of EQ,[11] or Emotional Quotient, is relevant here. Fundamentally, this is about an individual's ability to be emotionally aware and utilise their emotions in a positive and constructive way both to influence themselves and others purposefully, in a way that delivers appropriate and effective outcomes. Why is this so important? Traditionally, senior leaders have been elevated to their level based on their strong functional skills. In his acclaimed book, *What Got You Here Won't Get You There*, the eminent coach Marshall C. Goldsmith emphasises the importance of not relying too much on your functional skills, but putting more faith in your EQ.[12] As we progress, we develop new skills, but we need to be prepared to let go of some of those skills that have got us where we are in order to make space for the new ones that will serve us better.

I will indulge the reader with an anecdote to emphasise this point. I have a close associate who shared an interesting story with me to emphasise these points. My associate was working at C-Level for a significant international organisation, and he took a phone call from a regional leader one evening. The leader explained a situation whereby another senior leader was demotivating the team with very hostile and directive behaviour. This leader was strong at sales and business development, and the business figures were strong. However, the behaviour was totally destructive, was not allowing the team to blossom, and was hindering overall and future performance. The regional leader was brave in his approach, as his openness could have backfired. My associate made it clear on the call that he would follow up, but if the description was found to have no basis, then there could be serious consequences for the regional leader. The regional leader understood and had been prepared to take that level of personal risk. My associate did his research, and the description was substantiated with fact and verified observation. The C-Level leader phoned the potential 'bad actor' and suggested a meeting in London the following day. On the call the leader realised his behavioural challenges and determined that there was no way forward so tendered his verbal resignation. There was no requirement for a meeting. The key learning here is that quite often people subconsciously know their failings, but either do not know how to deal with them or are prepared to surface them without a trigger. The fact that our skills or lack of them can be self-limiting in terms of career is sometimes known as the Peter Principle.[13]

Avoiding concurrence!

Running significant different change programmes or concurrent initiatives can be a major challenge when enacting any cultural transformation. This may sound counter-intuitive, as one would expect a change programme to be multi-faceted with different but supporting elements. What I am talking about is where there are corporate-led programmes, which are intended to have significant outcomes on the way people work or behave, although with differing tangible results, but that also draw on the same resources. For example, I consulted with a major multinational in 2014 as it was rolling out a global behavioural safety programme. Once we got to the various sites, it was very clear that we were up against the challenge of multiple initiatives. Other consultants were helping the client with other change management programmes, and there was an overlap with ours. The shop-floor and first-line supervisors were already up to their 'capacity for change' and were clearly confused. For the purposes of clarity, in my experience, it is OK in complex organisations to work on different elements in parallel, but the border lines must be clearly defined, messages consistent and priorities clear. Clarity of purpose, and the communication thereof, are fundamental to the success of any change initiative.

I will now explain the last challenges that any leadership team would face with any cultural transformation as there are some deeper connections. I have briefly touched on team selection in the context of EQ, but I would like to develop that further in a way that helps to understand the challenges in any cultural transformation or change management programme. Change leaders must be multi-faceted, which not only includes functional competence and engagement skills, but also passion and drive. The latter qualities are critical, because any change programme for a large organisation, depending on its nature, can take from two to five years to be sustainable and properly embedded. It is important that the leaders and influencers have the drive and energy to see it through. I will cover some of the methodologies for maintaining this when I go deeper into coaching styles and theories.

To summarise, there are clearly numerous significant challenges when enacting any cultural transformation or change programme. Therefore, having all the elements in place to ensure the programme succeeds is fundamental and must be considered right from the start. Having a culture of regular coaching and appropriate support mechanisms will help significantly. Coaching needs to be totally integrated into the programme. One of the greatest challenges for coaches and coaching is that for it to be effective, it needs to be 'pull' not 'push', which means that those who are to be coached need to have the desire and open-mindedness to be coached. This is a challenge, because leaders often identify those who need to be coached based on their perceived gaps or failings. The client must buy into the change, be energised and be accountable for the overall result of the coaching process. This will give you some insights into why coaching is definitely 'pull' not 'push'. However, some staff do need a gentle 'nudge'. This will be covered later in the book, when I discuss the 60:20:20 model. I will cover coaching approaches in more detail as we progress through the book.

Listed below are some of the critical elements to be considered when facing the challenges of a transformation programme:

- 'Change' is difficult as humans are genetically programmed for routine and do not like to break it. In his article for the *New Scientist*, 'Why we are all creatures of habit', Mark Buchanan cites work done at MIT and reflections by the psychologist John Bargh of Yale University, that most humans react instinctively rather than follow their conscious intentions or deliberate choices.[14]
- The latest research indicates that approximately 70 per cent of all organisational change initiatives fail. This includes mergers and acquisitions, introductions of new technologies and changes in business processes.[15]

- Leaders and influencers often believe they are clear on the intent of the change programme, but it is usually not as clear as they think, and the vision is rarely communicated effectively.
- Getting the balance of skills correct on your leadership and transformation team is fundamental, and often biased to areas of functional competence rather than engagement or encouragement skills.
- Leaders can struggle to get the appropriate level of detail for a meaningful plan and can over-design, which leads to delays or procrastination at the start.
- Change programmes often get derailed due to competing initiatives or hidden conflicts.
- Responsibilities and accountabilities for executing change are not always clear.
- Planned timings are often unrealistic, especially at the start of a programme which in turn can create unnecessary stress and induce hidden delays.

There have been some catastrophic change management and cultural transformations, such as at Nokia, which failed to see the power of touch-screen technology. I will talk about change management models later in the book, but this would fall under a fear a failure category, but basically Nokia was not able to generate a sense of urgency. There was also the infamous scandal with Wells Fargo in 2016, when it created fake accounts as a means of meeting account quotas. This broke the rules on trust, transparency and authenticity. Specifically, here the adage goes, 'Rules drive behaviour and the wrong rules drive the wrong behaviour.'

There are some obvious key successes particularly in the tech and services sector. Companies like Amazon and Google keep reinventing themselves. As well as having engaged workforces, they are using the power of data and information to increase their market share and revenues. Over the years numerous blue-chip companies, even technology-based ones such as IBM, have had to reinvent themselves to survive. Companies have no other choice than to become more agile by harnessing data.

Context and nomenclature

I will use the terms 'change management' and 'cultural transformation' throughout the book, and it may seem that the terms are interchangeable, depending on the context of the work being done. For clarity, it is critical for the reader to understand the differences. I have referred to the term 'culture' earlier and presented the definitions. Most people find the concept of change easier to understand as, put simply, there is a difference in approach or problem outcome of a process. This can be quite transactional, but still involve all the key elements described earlier such as planning, visioning, execution, engagement, team building and communication. Historical and current change management models will be discussed in Chapter 5. Cultural transformation will involve some or all of the elements of change management, but it is more fundamental as it requires deeper thinking and inner work.[16] Inner work requires a level of personal risk, in that it will probably touch your personal values and beliefs, not just your transactional work or behaviour. It also requires a level of awareness among leaders and influencers, that it will take significant effort and buy-in from all those affected to deliver the transformation. Cultural transformation programmes will inevitably take longer for the reasons described above, but if executed properly will deliver sustainable and continual change. Simply put, organisations that have a culture of dealing with and continual change will find it much easier to enact significant future change. Paul Hunter, in his book *The Seven Inconvenient Truths of Business Strategy*, argues that having a formal strategy of continually evolving culture is the only way for organisations to survive in this VUCA world.[17]

Examples of change management programmes include:

- new ways of expense reporting
- productivity improvement programmes
- new marketing approaches
- new manufacturing techniques
- new accounting systems.

Examples of cultural transformations may include the following:

- e-learning
- use of customer relationship management (CRM) as opposed to different sales approaches
- organisational changes
- less hierarchical structures
- the use of personal power as opposed to command and control
- greater information and knowledge sharing.

There are many more, and both change management and cultural transformations will require coaching to a lesser or greater extent.

Key takeaways

Some key reflections on this chapter before the imperative for change is discussed in Chapter 3:

- There are more cultural transformation failures than there are successes, mainly driven by a lack of structure, foresight, communication and planning.
- Change management requires significant energy and effort, supported by strong leadership.
- Coaching has a key role to play. Later we will see the breadth and depth of support it can provide.
- Discipline, planning and structure are part of the key elements for success.
- Successful transformations require data, an engaged workforce and a 'no fear' mentality.

3 Imperative for change: Setting the productivity agenda, and securing buy-in

Productivity context and compromises

Why raise the question of productivity, when there are numerous reasons for cultural transformation or at least a change management programme? The reasons for a programme were covered at the end of Chapter 2, but productivity is critical for two reasons. First, in a rapidly changing and developing world, it is a key element in survival and longevity for any business. The quotation 'To stand still is to go backwards'[1] has always resonated with me. This links to my lean training, and the mantra of waste elimination. Second, for any change programme to be effective, it must be productive, i.e. deliver a result in a predetermined time. If it fails to do this, those that are either directly engaged with it, or are subjected to it, will get disaffected, turn off, not buy in and lose the value of the change. These are the reasons why the agenda must be set from the start.

For the purposes of this chapter, I will generally focus on the second element as it will have more resonance if I cover the efficiency of the transformation programme and make parallels where appropriate. There are plenty of books on productivity and 'lean'. In order to illustrate my points, I will assume that we are referencing a more transactional change management programme, or a cultural transformation programme with a clearly defined outcome in a predetermined time, as it is easier to link the concepts of productivity. Productivity is the rate at which a defined outcome can be delivered over time, or as a measure of the resources consumed (human, physical or financial) for a given output. Both these factors are relevant to a change programme and they will continue to be referenced as the influences on them are described. Coaching can and will have a huge influence on productivity.

At this point, it is worthwhile describing some of the coaching approaches and how they will influence the productivity of a change programme. There are numerous coaching styles and programmes, and we will touch on these later, but initially we will cover the demographics, and what coaching is not. Coaching differs significantly from training, consultancy and any form of knowledge transfer. It is about facilitating a team, group or individual to a desired end point. The critical point is that the end point is determined by the individual, group or team. I will discuss team coaching in Chapter 9. This is vital as it relates to the concept of pull vs. push, which will be discussed later. The push vs. pull lines can get a bit blurred with group and team coaching. One further element that can blur the lines for pull vs. push is that in organisations senior leaders can be assigned a coach, which can give the impression of push rather than pull. However, in these cases, executive coaches are usually assigned based on making client a better overall leader, rather than to deal with a specific issue or behaviour. This is one of the reasons why professional coaches are highly trained in facilitation and engagements skills and understand the importance of working to the client's agenda. In the case of private or personal coaching, then, the position is a lot clearer. Group coaching is generally where a cohort of individuals want to better themselves, and although they may not have the same or specific individual goals, they will get the benefit from the positive interactions created within the group. Team coaching is where the group has a common goal, and this is usually determined by the sponsor. This is often associated with sports, or functional areas such as sales and marketing. The coaching approach of NLP (neuro-linguistic programming) is used significantly within these two areas. Finally, we must also distinguish between coaching and mentoring. Mentoring will probably include coaching but is founded on the principle that the mentor or mentor coach has a similar or relevant experience to the client and will impart knowledge or share experience to aid progression.

In terms of setting the productivity agenda, a change management programme needs to have a clearly defined start point or 'Current State', an outcome or 'Final State' and a timeline, and some idea of resources. In fact, in consultant parlance, we describe this as a 'From' and 'To' exercise. As part of the early change project 'kick-off' and diagnostic phase, we will take the leadership through a 'From–To' exercise against some agreed diagnostic themes as a means of getting emotional buy-in and setting up success with enhanced leadership behaviours. This, as with every stage of the transformation, will require some supportive coaching in either group or individual format, whichever is the most appropriate.

This chapter is about the productivity agenda, something which will support the required change, in addition to acting as an Enabler and Accelerator[2] for it. As mentioned previously productivity can be defined in many ways. I described two of the simplest ones earlier. Ultimately this is about defining the improved business outcome, and working out how to achieve it either faster, better or less expensively (Figure 3.1). There is a great model of how these outcomes interact with one another (see Table 3.1). I first heard about it as project leader for a major construction project.

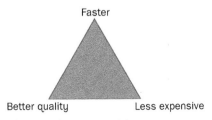

Figure 3.1 The faster, better, cheaper model

Table 3.1   Faster, better, cheaper alternatives

Cost	Quality	Speed	Functionality
Cheaper to produce	More durable	Faster to produce	More functions
Cheaper to ship	More robust	Supply chains shorter	Easier to use
Price competitive	Better branding	Faster to design	Connectivity
Selling costs cheaper	Greater market penetration	Faster to market	System integration
Advertising costs lower		Rapid research	
		Faster internal business processes	

Table 3.1 illustrates that it is only ever possible to have two out of the three attributes. It is possible to have a product made faster, and to better quality, but it is unlikely that it will be less expensive. It is possible to have it made faster, and less expensive, but it is unlikely to be of better quality. Finally, it may be possible to make it less expensive, and better quality, but it is unlikely to be made faster. However, with the last combination and modern robotics, it may be possible to have all three. The model is not perfect and a bit dated, but I find it useful to leaders and engineers if they think about outcomes and interactions at the start of any programme. Furthermore, it helps teams think about the unintended consequences of inappropriate combinations of outcomes. The more these are considered at the outset of a project, the greater the chance of success. This also ties in with the ethos of 'go slow to go fast'. So, let us look at some improved business outcomes.

Functionality, branding and quality will also drive significant price opportunities in addition to market penetration opportunities. This is far from an exhaustive list, but the above are legitimate business outcomes that require some level of change programme to implement. These also apply to the professional services sector as well as a physical product. In isolation or in combination, these will provide a macro business productivity improvement. It is critical that these are understood and explored at the start. NASA ran its FBC (Faster, Better, Cheaper) model, in the 1990s to reduce the time between space missions, showing that, under specially controlled conditions, with foresight these elements could be symbiotic. My aim is to highlight the principles and get people thinking deeper about the challenges.

Using pull

So, where does the coaching element come in? Exploring the above at a senior leadership level will require some level of facilitation and engagement, but it is possible that the change process to improve the business outcome may mean that a specific product or service that is owned by a team or department is dropped or significantly changed. This is where a skilled coach may be required to deal with either denial of the required changes, or acceptance that a leader must let go of something that he and his team have designed, built or nurtured. This is probably one of the most difficult areas of coaching as there will be a level of existing emotional buy-in as well as cognitive buy-in. There is another factor that makes this particularly difficult. Coaching in its purest form is 'pull' rather than 'push', i.e. the coaching agenda is set by the client. I will talk later in the book about similarities between coaching and productivity thinking with push vs. pull models, but the same principles apply. In 'pull' manufacturing models, production runs are determined by customer purchase rates, or 'Takt' rates.[3]

In this case, the client may need to get a 'nudge' either directly or indirectly from the programme leader or senior influencer. In my days in corporate real estate as head of UK Facilities Management, I regularly used to attend strategy meetings in Geneva, where we would discuss developing the European business and performance, and the team would struggle to move forward because one of the leaders found it difficult to let go of a work area or concept, because they were heavily invested in it. Marshall C. Goldsmith talks a lot about this in his book *What Got You Here Won't Get You There*,[4] the main tenet being that people can reach the level of their own incompetence by not embracing change, and more importantly can change by shedding things they do not need. This is particularly true of people who have got where they are through functional competence. In certain cases, this is very difficult to overcome. I know from my own engineering career, it was very difficult to understand that I no longer had to know all about the aspects of engineering or feel the need to share all of my knowledge as I moved up the management hierarchy. When I moved into FM (facilities management), I was hired because of that knowledge, to bring a level of structure or formality to the services sector that I oversaw. It took a bit of time for me to understand that in the case of contractor management, I did not need to be conversant in all the engineering aspects of the work, just structure and performance. I remember getting regular coaching sessions from my boss about this. It is a gradual process of realisation and leaders must show a level of patience as people go through the change. This is one of the advantages of employing a professional coach. Their formal training will give them the skills to facilitate the process quickly and effectively. Fortunately, modern technical and engineering curricula have more 'soft skills' awareness, business management and business process content in them. In my day, a significant proportion of the course was functional/technical with a bit of economics thrown in. I am currently coaching a future high potential client in a Middle Eastern chemical company who is sort of stuck in a paradigm whereby he feels that he needs to have the specific technical knowledge in the new area he is working in before he can truly have impact. We are working through this right now. I know he will get there, as it is clear he has the requisite EQ and has been selected as a high potential candidate for good reason. In these situations, a typical coaching approach would be to ask lots of open questions like 'Why', 'What', etc.

It is now clear that having clarity about the productivity agenda is as critical as 'visioning' to having a successful change programme or cultural transformation.

Some leaders may need coaching to get the buy-in. To deliver on the programme we will also need some alignment. Typically, the leadership team or steering committee will be made up of different functions to ensure the right level of transactional work is delivered between each critical milestone. The leadership team should have a chairperson, it will have a functional specialist, engineer, designer or creative person. The process will have stage gates or critical milestones, and as the programme will typically have additional resources, it will have a budget. It is likely that there could be some interim structural changes to the organisation, personnel moves or job real-location. HR and financial leaders should be on the programme leadership team. Even though the team members will have specific roles, they must be aligned to the common vision and demonstrate passion for the change to deliver the result. Team selection is critical because it will be not only about functional competence, but also about diversity, deep thinking, EQ, resilience, determination and an ability to hit the critical milestones. Ideally, a significant proportion of these skills will come from a reasonable proportion of the team members, but it is not necessary that all the team members have them and arguably it is not desirable. This is where team selection will be critical. As both an experienced consultant and coach I regularly must guide on the formation of critical change teams and help define the selection criteria. Furthermore, I am asked to facilitate the early formation meetings to set up quick alignment and help set the productivity agenda. I will come to this later.

Before we come to individual selection criteria, let us think about team selection criteria. This is a process that often gets lost in the excitement of a new programme. In certain cases, programme leaders fall into the positions accidentally, either through functional competency or seniority. Certain countries such as Germany create a culture where management training is part of leaders' development. This is one way in which this situation of the 'accidental manager' can be mitigated.

Project management

It is at this point in any programme I remind myself of a very cynical but sadly often realistic view of programme development that I became aware of in the early stages of my engineering career. Aptly named the five-step model, it is structured along the lines of the typical stages of an engineering project, as shown in Figure 3.2.

The 'cynical' version is shown in Figure 3.3. Aside from the humour, and the fact there is a level of cynicism which clearly should be avoided on a programme, it is a

Figure 3.2 The project management journey

| Stage 1–Excitement and euphoria | Stage 2–Disagreement and despondency | Stage 3–Hunt for the guilty | Stage 4–Blame the innocent | Stage 5–Glory for the uninvolved |

Figure 3.3 The alternative project management journey

timely reminder of why programmes can fail and often do fail. I remind myself the reason for this is twofold. First, as coaches we are taught to 'anchor', which is a mindfulness trick whereby we can stay steadfast in the face of adversity. This model is a trigger for me to anchor, and hopefully coach in a way that avoids these pitfalls. Second, as a leader or a coach this raises my awareness to look for, or be aware of, potential behaviours that could mark the onset of these stages. Finally, by sharing Figure 3.3 with a leadership team, it can inject some humour, which always helps support a long tough journey, and it sets a baseline for the team members to avoid any individual behaviours that could trigger these approaches in the programme. I will cover the actual stages of a change management programme in Chapter 5.

As an aside, I am a big fan of an appropriate, with the emphasis on appropriate, level of 'trench humour' on a programme, as it can bring identity to the team and serve as light relief. I recall being at the inception of a large client delivery for an industrial client in Indonesia back in 2013. I have touched on the power of team diversity before, but in global management consultancy, as with large engineering projects, people with a wide range of skills and diverse backgrounds naturally get thrown together, which is immensely powerful if harnessed correctly. Programme kick-off, especially when away from home for significant periods of time can lead to extreme stress and friction. In Indonesia, we had a reasonable kick-off, akin to stage 1 of the 'cynical model' in Figure 3.3. Unfortunately, I had a major stomach upset at the start of the project and was laid up in my hotel room over the weekend, with colleagues passing my medications under the door to avoid being contaminated. Good consultants only get ill at weekends. The one thing any consultant dreads is getting ill while away from home, and the unhealthy cocktail of long hours, sleep deprivation, too much drink and fast food does not help. There is a great Dilbert cartoon entitled 'Booze Muhkidney',[5] a skit on two global consulting firms, which illustrates this aspect of management consulting perfectly.

The second week of this consulting engagement we were all summoned to a series of global conference calls, where the new director of global consulting was to give us a rousing speech about the new consulting structure, business rates, charging methodologies, etc. As part of this speech, specifically mentioning four key roles and using a music analogy, he described the regional business development directors as the new 'rock stars' of the business as they were managing the pipelines. He went on to describe the 'solution architects' as the creators or song-writers, and the project managers as the 'roadies' who kept it all together, moving it along in the right direction and on time. There was a passing mention of the fourth role of delivery consultant who did the work in the field, with virtually no recognition. Ninety per cent of those in the room were delivery consultants. There was a very pregnant pause, with some blank looks and, when the speech was over, some muted laughter and a lot of cynicism. Here we were cranking out work in front of the client in the trenches and no recognition. On reflection, I am sure the aim was to emphasise the importance of the other new roles, but when giving a speech of that nature, think about the audience, another area where coaching can help. The team got through it with our customary trench humour and made frequent reference to establishing a 'consultants' union' as a means of keeping us going.

The director moved on not long after that. I do recall sending a note some time later to the new VP with the heading, 'View from the Trenches'. I am happy to say, on the back of this he reached out, we had a chat and I was able to share my perspectives based on that harmony.

So back from the segue to thinking around team selection. To get the correct team, we need to consider the outputs and characteristics of the combined team. It is important to understand that with the selection of a steering team, the skills required may not be closely linked to the actual design of the system change. So, for example, if the systemic change is related to the greater adoption of IT and automation, the steering team needs to have an outline understanding of the technology that will be adopted, but not necessarily loaded with IT specialists. In this example, the programme will involve a level of cultural transformation as well as change management. The IT specialists will be involved as a separate design and execution sub-team.

Steering teams

What would be the typical composition of a steering team? At this point we need to consider the characteristics and behaviours of the team based on the key outputs and activities. If we first look at the outputs, then these can be loosely considered as:

- Demonstrate passion for the change or transformation.
- Ensure that the project scope is maintained, i.e. not reduced or expanded.
- Challenge the 'Transformation Manager' to meet deadlines and budgets.
- Provide guidance and feedback to the execution teams.
- Provide formal and informal mentoring as required.
- Provide key stakeholder input and guidance.
- 'Gatekeep' the project or programme.
- Act as 'Governors' for the programme.
- Have the ability to take a strategic view and drill down into the detail when required.

Depending on the nature of the change required, these may vary slightly, but these are the core outputs and activities.

The steering team does not have a primary role in providing oversight expertise, but functioning expertise can be helpful in the context of mentoring. So, if we move on a level, let us list the capabilities, characteristics and behaviours of the team members, building on what is described above:

- Leadership based on knowledge, experience and engagement.
- The ability to show people (staff) the way.
- Strong conceptual capacity.
- Strong cognitive skills.
- The ability to process significant volumes of information and put them into context.
- The ability to challenge constructively and hold others to account.
- Ability to demonstrate authenticity and trust.
- A role model for the behaviours expected of others.
- Understanding of the principles of good governance.
- Good listening skills.
- Knowledge of when to interject and add value.

You may be thinking that the characteristics just described are those of a 'board'. This is because the role of the steering team or group is very similar to that of a board, whether it is a company board or board of school governors.

In the early 2000s, I was given the role of programme/project manager for a significant construction project in Spain. This was not in chemicals production, but in facilities management and real estate. This project went beyond the basics of a project as it was linked to significant cultural change in the organisation. The company was bringing several different support functions, including IT, HR and Finance, together into a common European service centre. This was to be a cultural shift for the company, as it meant that regional and country HR support would be reduced significantly with the creation of this central support hub. This would not only impact the staff involved, but also the staff that the functions traditionally supported in the countries. As a service centre this meant that it was to be open plan, with minimal offices and breakout space, which was a departure from the company norm. Staff had to learn how to interact with one another in different ways, and the design was critical. This went beyond a typical building construction project with a project manager, engineers and designers. The correct transition to this way of working was essential, and because the centre was to incorporate a level of Global Finance, there needed to be power back-ups and dedicated servers. The net result was that we had a programme steering team to guide the project with numerous stakeholders, which resembled a steering group similar to that of a significant change programme (Figure 3.4). In addition to the functional stakeholders, whose staff was going to be resident, the steering team comprised senior real estate leaders and the site director. The location was a large manufacturing site with spare land. There was a recognition that doubling the site population by adding one building to a series of manufacturing plants was going to present some additional cultural challenges. For these reasons, I visited an IBM service centre in the UK, along with the local head of construction and the site director, to get some insights into how a service centre building would work effectively.

Figure 3.4 Steering team

My manager was the regional real estate leader and acted as the conduit between me and the steering team. The HR function brought in professional coaches and additional trainers to guide the new way of working, and help staff understand their new roles. It was not just the new HR staff who needed to be guided and trained, but regional managers who were losing their local HR support. The coaching approaches here need to be varied depending on the situation of the specific demographics. First, coaching in its purest form is about pull rather than push. The agenda is clearly with the clients. However, in this scenario, there is a clear outcome or aim that must be achieved, so there is a push element. The coaching skill will be around getting the message across, while building trust, and being authentic and engaging. One of the coaching techniques that could be employed here is 'seed planting'. This is where the coach plants a seed which is related to the desired outcome. The client or client makes the connection in a positive way, so that they can move forward. This is one of many techniques to use. There are many others that trigger taking accountability or removing fear. This is where the skill of the coach is to identify which approach is most appropriate based on the initial dialogue. Flushing out the concerns, barriers and fears, then facilitating a process to the outcome is the next stage. If there are common problems around buy-in for a change, then coaching could be done at the team level. Either way, a good coach will ensure there is a clear agenda for the next session and hold the individuals or team accountable for their results.

The service centre also had to be multilingual, and new graduates were being hired from all over Europe for HR. This also meant a blend of regional cultures were being imported who had to find a way of blending not only into the Spanish culture, but also into a manufacturing site culture. It required compromise and understanding on all sides. In fact, the net result was a blended culture, which is now very strong.

The system worked well and all those on the steering team had the attributes previously described. The project was brought in on time, and only 4 per cent above overall budget. The facility is still functioning today.

Team diversity

A few reflections on team diversity at this stage in the book; again I will talk in more detail about this later, as it is very relevant to delivery work. The simple model

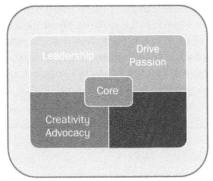

Outer Annulus represents Increased Bandwidth

Figure 3.5 Team diversity

shown in Figure 3.5 shows some of the competencies and capabilities described earlier. The characteristics of 'change champions' or 'change agents' will be discussed later when we look at programme execution in detail. There is a special set of attributes which are diverse that sets change agents apart. Having one or two on the steering team can be additive.

Diverse teams deliver more than their constituent parts. Furthermore, diversity goes beyond gender, ethnicity, culture or sexual orientation, but includes thought, or, better put, the way people think. Neurodiversity is a prevalent topic currently, as it not only helps with creativity and inclusivity, but also can increase the overall skill level of any team as the boundaries are pushed.[6] Neurodivergent people think in different ways to what is considered the population norm, and many have conditions that place them on the autism spectrum. They usually have unique skills. A multi-disciplinary team whose members are neurodiverse will have a working envelope greater than the sum of its constituent parts. Neurodiversity is beginning to find its way into the board room and leadership teams, with powerful results. A significant number of successful entrepreneurs are considered to be neurodiverse.

Some further final reflections on programmes in the context of productivity. I will talk more about lean approaches later in the book, but this is a journey. Within the framework we use approaches such as value stream mapping, which looks at the value-adding steps from a 'current state' to a 'future state'. The same thinking could be applied to a cultural transformation or change management. There are other similarities such as the need for timelines and resource planning.

Coaching context and learning points

There are some key learning points from this chapter in the context of setting up for success. For the purpose of understanding at this point and in the later chapters, I use the word coaching in a wider context, which covers the roles of internal coaches, external coaches (contractors), leadership coaches, team coaches and executive coaches. Professional coaches can fulfil these roles, depending on the work context. However, any coach needs to be realistic about their own bandwidth before taking on a client or clients. The reader should apply this understanding when assimilating their thinking and applying perspective. I will discuss in more detail the key aspects of team and individual coaching in Chapter 9.

Key takeaways

- Understanding the productivity agenda for any transformation programme is critical. There are many ways that productivity can be defined. An ethos of productivity will get early traction and alignment because individuals and teams always want to do better, and generally like challenging the status quo.
- Depending on the size and nature of the programme, consider setting up a steering team. Keeping a steering team separate from the execution team can help with governance and overall performance.
- Selecting the correct team at the start of the transformation is critical, and identifying change champions who have the appropriate characteristics and exemplify the right behaviours will enable and accelerate the process of change.
- The skills required to drive and deliver a change programme will differ from the functional skills required to execute the detailed work.
- Coaching can have impact right at the start of the transformation programme. Coaching is not only for the execution team.
- Coaches, irrespective of context, should always think about 'pull' as a means of ensuring the client objective is met, whether it is an individual or a team.
- The old rules do not apply. Changing geopolitical situations are driving the need for changing company cultures specifically around the need for transparency. People now are more value-driven. If we do what we always did, companies will struggle.
- Productivity improvement is a continuous journey and needs energy with coaching support.

4   Cultural challenges: Changing culture is not easy

Cultural context

We would not be able to talk about change management or cultural transformation without describing different cultures, their specific characteristics, and how they are embedded and influenced. Some definitions of culture were given in Chapter 2.

It is important before any transformation or change programme is initiated that the existing culture is properly understood. There are cultures that will support improvement and change and those that will stifle and hinder change. Let us look at some of the company cultures and their specific characteristics. So far, I have not really touched on emotional intelligence, or EI, but this is a good time to do so because our traditional thinking around a performance culture is that it is action-oriented. These cultures tend to be more transactional, rather than transformational. If we are going to drive change, and have a business that is continually evolving, then we need a combination of both transaction and transformation. Paul Hunter, in his book *The Seven Inconvenient Truths of Business Strategy*,[1] postulates that business culture needs to be continuously evolving and have its own ecosystem. The key point is this challenges the existing thinking, that a business culture needs to move from A to B. I liken the position to 'Darwinism',[2] i.e. survival of the most adaptable. The VUCA environment (volatile, uncertain, complex, ambiguous) means that every business change is working at a faster rate, assuming businesses want to remain competitive. In short, this means business agility.

Agility

However, this is not just about using agile working[3] techniques. Agile is a type of project management process, mainly used for software development, where demands and solutions evolve through the collaborative effort of self-organising and cross-functional teams and their customers. The agile approach has had some success in improving productivity and time to market, but it does have some shortfalls. Some in the software development community argue that it misses a key element, that is the lifecycle review. I would like to argue that lean, agile and other approaches are not necessarily working cultures but approaches or sub-system cultures. One of the attributes of a continually developing culture is the requirement for challenge and curiosity. I believe in the following quotation, 'Past performance is not a predictor of future greatness.' In the recruitment arena, companies are not just looking for those with strong previous performance, but those with latent intelligence, curiosity and the ability to self-learn and self-start. Results in one area are no guarantee of results in another company, but conventionally that is what recruiters have been looking for. This is critical because the smartest people can adapt to a constantly changing environment, as happens in physical evolution and Darwin's theory of the survival of the fittest. These are the kind of leaders and participants which will support an evolving culture.

Effective leadership

The most effective leaders will not only be able to work strategically or with details when required, but also understand the required blend between transactional and transformational work. The most effective change leaders and coaches understand when to view from the 'helicopter' (being strategic) and when to view in the 'weeds' (analysing the detail) (Figure 4.1).

In the same way they blend the action-oriented transactional work with the more radical transformational work .This is a unique skill that generally has been honed with experience, or in some unique cases exists in the formative years of some very talented leaders, usually with high levels of emotional intelligence. So, what is the connection with coaching and company culture? These leaders have a good sense of what a 'company culture' is and can smell it. Why is this important? This is important because those in leadership roles who have these skills can see and smell

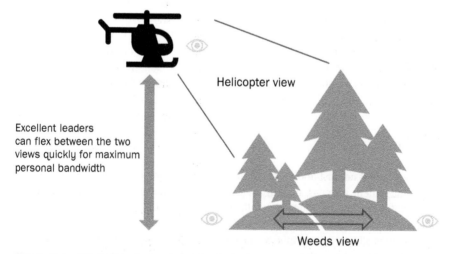

Figure 4.1 The helicopter and weeds views

things that are going wrong. They are also not afraid to be different, which means they will take a level of personal risk, i.e. putting their heads above the parapet to make the appropriate changes. As I have alluded to before, these are also the characteristics of a strong coach. The intention of this book is to guide the reader on how to build context and make connections using examples, not be a manual on coaching. The reader should go deeper into each topic, such as EI as an example for greater understanding. It is worth noting numerous books have been written on EI.

A good example of such a leader was Samuel Palmisano at IBM.[4] In an interview for the *Harvard Business Review*, he describes how, although business was good at IBM in the early 2000s, it had lost its way. The business was overly bureaucratic in a complex and diverse way, which had stifled some end-to-end thinking. He talks about the fact that each business unit had its own P&L (Profit & Loss) section, so when they needed to come up with integrated business solutions for clients, this had become limiting as each business was trying to drive its own P&L without thinking about the overall business impact for IBM. He was smart enough to realise that the Chief Financial Officer was thinking the same way, so they embarked on an initiative to change the situation, even though this required significant effort. To enact this requires a level of 'values-based thinking', in this case the value of looking at the whole rather than the constituent parts. Furthermore, he embarked on a very radical approach, where he designed and implemented a three-day interactive online company feedback/discussion session on company values, as he had recognised a strong company culture, based on the initial values of its founder, but also the need for change in the modern, more dynamic and competitive business environment. Inappropriate systems and bureaucracy were holding the business back. It was impossible to work effectively in the new marketplace without a significant change. However, he was also smart enough and sufficiently in touch with the organisation to recognise that the company had been founded on values, and that connection to values resonated strongly with the staff. This had also been evident when Lou Gerstner had taken the helm of the company in more troubled times, back in 1993. Nobody wanted the company to go under. This was the idea for the inception of the 'Values Jam' interactive session. He recalls in this interview that although there was some negativity online, there were also some positive and constructive comments. He read all the comments, and printed them out, when the exercise was complete. He also commented, even though he was travelling and jetlagged while the system was live. He had teams of analysts working with software doing keyword searches and population statistical work to help them derive some new company values. After considerable effort, the net effect was to come up with three new key values: (1) dedication to every clients' success; (2) innovation that matters – for our company and the world; and (3) trust and personal responsibility in all relationships. These were not radically different from the company founders' values, which were Respect, Customer, Excellence and Innovation, and in fact had some common themes, but were more action-based, less nebulous and resonated in the modern business environment. This was a radical but very clever approach, because he managed to maintain a common thread in a well-established company that was not only respected by the business community but by its employees, and also managed to break the mould with the 'Values Jam' approach, which a lot of people considered would fail or backfire. In this way he exemplified some of the key traits, behaviours and approaches of effective change leaders highlighted earlier. A considerable number of senior executives and change leaders become mentors and coaches.

Company cultures

I will go on to talk about company cultures, and how through coaching, leadership and change management, they can be influenced over time. I will revert to some personal examples based on my earlier career experience. I started my engineering career in petrochemicals for BASF, which is still one of the largest petrochemical companies today. I had an enjoyable experience, with lots of early support from other engineers and mentors. It was a very collaborative culture which was epitomised by the fact nobody ever wanted anyone to fail. I was lucky enough to do some very interesting and technically challenging projects. In the early days I worked with both R&D in the German HQ and a top professor on particle/catalyst flow dynamics in fluidised beds at Bradford University. Our work was both development-based and practical. The work was a success and led to a design change in the cyclone 'diplegs' in the fluidised bed acrylonitrile fluid bed reactors at the triennial plant general shutdown. The modification worked and the catalyst losses were significantly reduced downstream. On the back of this, I was given another project which was both technically challenging and had the potential to help transform reactor performance (yield) on a long-term basis. BASF had taken over the site from another large company, Monsanto, and was not afraid to invest money in R&D as it developed the business. I was given the opportunity to build a full vertical-scale pilot reactor, which was to be integrated with the main two production reactors. This was to be a 1/15th diameter scale of the full reactor, which would mimic the fluid bed dynamics of the full-scale reactor, because it was full height but only using a fraction of the catalyst inventory. Testing and developing catalysts for yield improvements in a production reactor is an expensive business. Prior to this, catalysts had only ever been tested in the laboratory, which would not give the full picture. I embarked on this exciting project and even visited the US to see a similar reactor and gather as much data as I could. There were some interesting safety and technical challenges, but these were overcome and two years later the reactor started its test and commissioning runs. It was a success, and the R&D team went about the catalyst appraisal programme. At that specific time this was the most significant and expensive project on site, so the leadership team were looking for my next move. I was offered the chance of being the Engineering Manager for a different division in the UK Midlands region. Never one to miss an opportunity, I took it.

A more challenging culture

I was moving to a significantly older site that manufactured inks and automotive paints. The infrastructure and culture at the two sites could not have been more different. The former was clean, well maintained with an air of order and control, and the latter was the exact opposite. I had no idea of what I had walked into. You instinctively know things are going to be different, but never have a real idea of how bad they are. I vividly recall struggling to sleep as I relocated, fearful of what could happen from a safety perspective. My intuition held true and we had a couple of relatively serious near misses in the first eight weeks. The cultures could not have been more different. One was open, transparent and supportive, and the other the complete opposite with a level of suspicion and mild hostility. I even thought that my team was viewing me with some reticence as they considered me to be the corporate spy. I had begun to rue the decision, but I had to move forward. Fortunately, another new but more experienced manager took on the safety role. We started to identify the physical site issues, and get the financial and human resources in place to deal with the infrastructure and safety issues. There were also upgrade projects under way. I led both the engineering and maintenance functions. The maintenance supervisor was also a difficult character and gave me little support, and it was clear that he was not considered a leader by his team. We also had suspicions about potential inappropriate business relations with local repair contractors. We later found evidence of this, and he exited the company. This was a difficult time for me, because the deeper we looked, the more we found. Fortunately, the engineering manager from my previous site made a surprise visit and took me for lunch. He had the foresight to realise that I would be having a tough time due to the local politics, in addition to the state of the site. This was my first exposure to coaching. The approach was both purposeful and empathetic. He also agreed to be my mentor, which was a huge relief. It was good to know that I had senior support in my corner. We progressed through the projects, sorted out the infrastructure, improved the safety culture. I waited six months before I appointed a new maintenance supervisor, which added a huge load to my daily work. It was the best decision I made, because I could get to know the team, bring some focus back to them and raise their profile.

I moved on to another role at a Total UK subsidiary, and after two years was able to reflect that we had achieved a lot, at the previous site, in what had started out as a more hostile culture. At one point, I was even threatened by a fire installation contractor with a 20-inch wrench when I challenged the validity of a pressure test on a sprinkler system. However, one of my greatest career moments was when my senior mechanical technician came to me on my last day and said, 'We did not know how to take you at first, we thought you were the corporate spy from the big plant. However, we appreciate what you have done, and you restored pride in the department, supported us when we needed it and recognised our work.' I moved on to a bigger role (TOTAL) at another paints plant, but soon realised the culture was similar.

In my small way, I had shifted the culture within my department from one of resignation to pride. During my tenure, I had many coaching sessions with my peers and team, which included both 'softer' discussions, such as those which were encouraging, and harder ones which were around the acceptance of new approaches and initiatives. For example, the harder ones were on supporting the implementation of many new critical initiatives, such as new safety and operational procedures to both drive performance and mitigate risk. After proper processing and alignment, these were 'zero option' discussions. This was my early exposure to 'resistance to change'. The resistance came from the position of, 'We have always done it this way' and 'What do you know about paint manufacture?' Initially this was a challenge for me for many reasons. I was relatively young and inexperienced as a manager. Furthermore, I was used to a culture of collaboration from my previous experience in petrochemicals and, to use the words of John Kotter, 'creating a guiding coalition'.

I use this example to show that, sometimes, the requirement for mental toughness and resilience during implementation gets forgotten in the less bureaucratic and hierarchical business world today. I regularly remind myself that this environment was only in the early 1990s so it was less than 30 years ago. I would have not said that the environment was openly hostile, but it was mildly subversive, until the point we got traction with the initiatives, and effectively 'critical mass'. The 'softer' discussions I described earlier refer to the need to encourage your own team and guide them in the new initiatives. I remember many a late-night coaching discussion with shifts, when the core day work had been completed and the volatility of work had calmed down. I quickly learned that the way you deliver the message, whether soft or hard, is as important as the message itself. I will come to this in a bit, but I would first like to talk a little more about getting traction.

The 80:20 rule

There has been a considerable amount written on the 80:20 rule and from a 'lean' perspective this is a founding principle. The 80:20 rule, sometimes known as the Pareto principle, is used to describe situations where 80 per cent of consequences come from 20 per cent of the causes and vice versa. This 'universal truth' about the imbalance of inputs and outputs is what became known as the 80:20 rule. While it does not always come to be an exact 80:20 ratio, this imbalance is often seen in various business cases, for example 20 per cent of the sales reps generate 80 per cent of total sales. Because of this context, it is sometimes used as a means of avoiding procrastination or diminishing returns.

Some exponents will say that this is an excellent approach to dealing with procrastination or what can be defined as 'postponed perfection', i.e. the means of delaying critical work in the pursuit of excellence. I was even mentored during the writing of this book to write it from beginning to end to the best of my ability and standards, then critique and rewrite it chapter by chapter in the pursuit of excellence. The latter approach is postponed perfection, and many an author has failed to hit a deadline with this approach.

I recall delivering coaching sessions and workshops at a major Russian client in 2012 on the 80:20 rule, as we were losing momentum on the change programme. With a strong technical and process background, certain teams were stuck in the 100/0 paradigm, where they were delaying the start of certain key change initiatives, due to not having all the data available.

Intraculturality

There was another contributory factor in addition to chasing perfection: 'uncertainty avoidance', a common issue in culture or change management programmes. Geert Hofstede refers to this element as one of the determinates in his six dimensions of 'intraculturality'.[5] Different regional and country cultures have different appetites for risk, and this is clearly exemplified in the Russian culture. We know from the definitions of cultures that these are defined as collective beliefs, values and behaviours, so a macro representation of this data will manifest itself in the people and communities. In Hofstede's analysis of cultural values, in Figure 4.2, Russia scores 95 whereas the USA and Qatar score 80 and 46 respectively.

I ran the workshops and the key message I elucidated was around differentiating between a management process, such as holding effective meetings, versus a technical or engineering process like designing an aeroplane wing, where the physical risk is considerably higher. I find targeted coaching and workshops can be very effective at getting over barriers such as critical thinking and will shift the culture. This type of work is essential in cultural transformation, as it can remove multiple barriers and act as a means of enabling and acceleration.[6] I also use this expression as a mental trigger for me to aid my own thoughts on traction. I even use it as a tag line in my own productivity consulting business. If I am having a particularly difficult time with procrastination, I think of another variant to get traction. I consider the 60:40 rule (in a non-standard context), whereby if you have roughly 60 per cent of the required information, you know which direction you are going or path to follow, and you can start immediately.[7]

Another concern I hear often, is 'If we go 80:20, what are the guarantees that we will get to 100 per cent or completion?' The truth is that there are no guarantees, just models and approaches. This type of feedback can indicate an 'Energy Blocker'[8] or

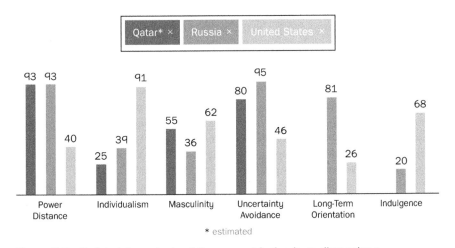

Figure 4.2 Hofstede's analysis of three countries' culture dimensions

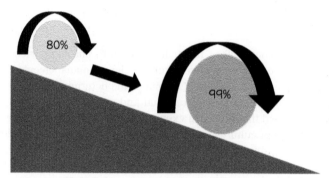

Figure 4.3 The 80:20 getting traction and gaining momentum model

'Self-imposed Paradigm'. One way I deal with these situations is by using a simple analogy of a snowball rolling down a snow-covered slide. As it rolls down the slide, it gets bigger as it gathers snow and increases its circumference (Figure 4.3). The increasing circumference can be likened to adding more energy as a means of getting closer to the goal. Furthermore, science tells us that larger-diameter wheels move more freely and can cover rough ground, increasing the chance of success. Figure 4.3 can be used for both individuals and groups, either in coaching or workshops.

That was one element of resistance to change, at either an individual or small group level, but let us now look at the macro picture, which again can relate to a company or regional culture.

Resistance to change

In my experience, there will always be some level of resistance to change. The reasons for this can be multi-faceted and I will cover them in more detail later in the book. However, I follow a simple heuristic when implementing change in a significant site or large organisation. It will not directly solve problems but will give those who are responsible for change a level of context and understanding of how the change is going to unfold, i.e. a level of preparedness, which is useful for both the client and the coach/consultant. I call this the 60:20:20 model (see Figure 4.4). When coaching and consulting, I only share this when the client asks, because sometimes there is very little resistance at the start, and there is no need to share it. Figure 4.4 illustrates the three phases that staff can go through as part of the cultural or change journey. The basic principles are simple. If the planned change makes sense, and the vision makes sense, then generally 60 per cent will buy in very quickly, leaving 40 per cent, split evenly between those who don't want to come on board and the 'don't knows'. Usually in the second stage, the 20 per cent don't knows move across to the 60 per cent relatively quickly, once they see that 60 per cent are positive. This is akin to not wanting to be left out, almost 'me too'. This is sometimes referred to as the 'bandwagon effect' in psychological journals and comes under the category of cognitive

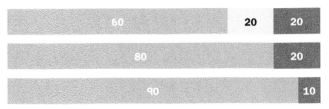

Figure 4.4 The 60:20:20 traction model for change

or decision-making/behavioural biases. Very few people generally sit on the fence. This creates the new critical mass of 80:20. In stage 3, the remaining 20 per cent begin to feel very isolated, and usually 10 per cent of the remainder flip across to join the 80 per cent to create 90 per cent. The remaining 10 per cent can be considered the hard-core dissenters. At this point, leadership is left with the decision of what to do with them. More may come onside, but the key point is that you recognise the position. It will depend very much on the roles of the remainder in terms of approach. There may be an opportunity to coach, if they are pivotal to success, or you find roles for them that will not negatively impact the change.

Messaging

There are many solid and proven good management practices for delivering harder or tough messages. These include being factual, data-driven, avoiding assumptions, being calm, avoiding inappropriate emotion, and not being overly friendly. I will cover feedback and difficult conversations later in the book. To provide further context on coaching sessions and improve the early coaching dialogue, I would like to touch on another topic I have found successful. I have also delivered this as part of coach training.

In any coaching session, the two most critical things are authenticity and trust. Sometimes people confuse the two, but they are different. Authenticity is about personal congruence, and showing up as you truly are, which is critical as a coach. Professional coach training puts a heavy emphasis on this, as those who are not authentic will struggle. Some argue this is a prerequisite for coaching. Trust is different, and is all about the relationship building, which again is critical for effective coaching. In NLP considerable emphasis is put on this with the RESOLVE model. I look at this in the context of when to use EI and when to use processing skills. There are psychological models that talk about the left and right brains, or the lateralisation of the brain function. Historically it has been believed that the right brain controls more of the feelings or emotional responses, and the left controls the cognitive processes. Although this is a simplistic view and is being challenged by some neuroscientists, it can be a useful characterisation from a heuristic perspective. We can coach for change and performance, but it requires advocating a good balance of left and right brain. Once my students understand the classification, I ask them the question. 'Ideally which part of the brain would you use to start a coaching

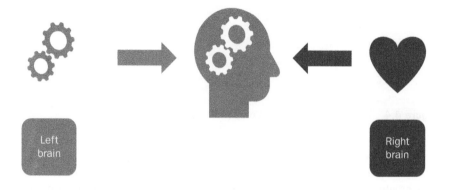

Figure 4.5   Heart vs. head and left and right brains

dialogue?' The answer is always correct, which is the right side because we need to build trust before we get into any cognitive processing. Using our EI will help us build trust at the start. Once trust is established, then the cognitive work can start, and that will build an effective coaching relationship. I have never really applied it to group or team coaching sessions formally, but it is possible to do so. If you look at the most engaging speakers, or those who do TED talks, generally they engage with their audiences early, by tapping into the emotions.

My next role was at another coatings plant back in the Midlands, and I soon realised after the corporate acquisition by DuPont that sometimes it is the industry cultures that are more similar than company corporate cultures. I learned that there was greater similarity in cultures between DuPont Automotive Coatings and BASF Coatings than their petrochemical counterparts. I was eternally grateful for the early coaching I received. As well as countries, regions and companies, industries can have cultures too.

Cultural models

I propose having another look at the definitions of organisational or company culture. These definitions characterise company cultures from a strategic and holistic perspective with the basis being communal behaviours and assumptions. Companies or organisations can even have their own subcultures which we will cover later in the book. I have already mentioned some definitions from culture and change management experts such as John Kotter.

Ravasi and Schultz (2006) characterise organisational culture as a set of shared assumptions that guide behaviours.[9] The pattern of such collective behaviours and assumptions is what is taught to new organisational members as a way of perceiving, and even thinking and feeling. Thus organisational culture affects the way people and groups interact with one another, with clients and with stakeholders. In addition, organisational culture may affect how much employees identify with an organisation. Schein (1992), Deal and Kennedy (2000), and Kotter and Heskett (1992) advanced the idea that organisations often have very differing cultures as well as subcultures.[10] Although a company may have its 'own unique culture', in larger organisations there are sometimes co-existing or conflicting subcultures because each subculture is linked to a different management team. These also show in different functions, e.g. marketing versus design.

As mentioned earlier, industries can have subcultures, and so can sites in the same organisation and the same businesses. This can often depend on the history, growth and style of leadership.

I will take a deeper look at company cultures from a couple of different perspectives. First, we will look at the eight cultural styles or characteristics, as defined by Boris Groysberg, Jeremiah Lee, Jesse Price and J. Yo-Jud Cheng in their *Harvard Business Review* article, 'The leader's guide to corporate culture'.[11] They analysed 230 companies and 1,300 executives comprehensively and found eight distinct culture styles. I will then look at the four Corporate Cultural Dimensions as described by the OCAI (Organizational Cultural Assessment Instrument). The aim in this chapter is to raise awareness of different types of cultures in organisations, and touch on how coaching can have an impact. This will not be a practical guide on how to coach in each one. At this point, I am not going to cover hostile or hierarchical organisations, but will in due course.

Eight characteristics of culture

This section is informed by the eight characteristics model, which I would encourage readers to look at it in Groysberg et al.'s article online. Broadly speaking, this model is divided into four quadrants. In the first (north-east), caring and purpose are situated on the axis between interdependence and flexibility. In the second (south-east), order and safety are situated between the axes of interdependence and stability, authority and results in the south-west quadrant between the stability and independence axes. The final quadrant, as we progress clockwise (north-west), comprises employment and learning between the axes of independence and flexibility.

The eight characteristics are:

1. Purpose
2. Caring
3. Order
4. Safety
5. Authority
6. Results
7. Enjoyment
8. Learning.

Groysberg et al.'s article provides a lot more detail as it goes into great depth on the culture styles and outcomes, with the context being that senior leaders have two key levers for maintaining and improving organisational effectiveness, which are culture and strategy. The authors discuss five key insights from their in-depth research. They survey the considerable literature from leading experts such as Schein, Schwarz and Hofstede. They also illustrate that culture can be shifted and improved, even though some leaders avoid tackling the challenges of a certain culture, or the ones that are not serving the business. This is where a co-ordinated coaching programme can have impact. The critical point being that if you know your start point, which can be done by a simple assessment, you will find it easier to reach your end goal. If we refer to one of the key tenets of Paul Hunter's book,[12] the business strategy should be a developing culture. When I see these, I do not just see these as cultures, but almost as attributes, orientations and, in certain cases, linked to behavioural types. In the case of the OCAI four dimensions (see Figure 4.6), these are more akin to business approaches, but there are some similarities, particularly in that both models are segmented by quadrants.

In Groysberg et al.'s structure, we can see that the north–south axis represents flexibility moving towards stability and independence moving to interdependence. Furthermore, they discuss the way in which people interact, and how people respond to change. Understanding these factors in any organisation can be critical to coaching success. It is worthwhile noting that there is a distinct difference between independence and interdependence. The latter is built on the former, but has a stronger element of unconditional collaboration, teamwork and support. This is sometimes characterised as 'my brother's keeper' where staff look out for one another. So, where the two cultures of purpose and caring reside, we can see a high level of interdependence in a caring culture, with a high sense of purpose with reflecting the responsiveness to change. In the second quadrant we see the cultural styles of order and safety. Order is reflected by the level of interdependence, i.e. that individuals and teams are self-sufficient, and stability is reflected with the need for safety. If we take the third quadrant, we can see an orientation for results being reflected by a level of independence. In the final and fourth quadrant, we see that independence supports a level of enjoyment in the culture, and flexibility supports a culture for learning. The beauty of this structure is that it has sense and logic, even for those who do not have a strong psychological background, and it is extremely helpful for leaders. What I like further about this model is the way that the cultural styles fit well with the 'compass points'. If we take the northern tip, flexibility is a key attribute for cultural styles of learning and purpose. As we work round the compass, caring and order are totally congruent with interdependence, the environment of authority and safety create stability, and finally independence should foster a level of interdependance.

Some of these attributes may exist in an organisation, and some of them may be desired by leadership as a means of developing the business or the organisation. For instance, at a time of significant organisational structural change, an organisation would be looking for flexibility within its systems and staff. After an acquisition and incorporation of another business, it would be looking for stability. For a new or immature organisation, it may be creative and directive, but with a desire to move to independence, as productivity demands the staff be more self-sufficient. It is important to remember that, if independence is required, then processes and systems must be developed or be in the process of development. If we follow this through, and business pressure puts stress on staff numbers, then there will be a desire for staff to be more interdependent, i.e. support one another, look after one another and take on more. In times of staff reduction, organisations need to be actively caring, and ensure order is maintained.

Unfortunately, I have been in the unenviable position of having to manage site closures and staff exits. During these times it was essential we had an appropriate sense of caring and we had to attempt to maintain good order to run the site safely and protect the people. My experience (Minworth site, closed in 2000) showed that attention to detail had to be heightened to maintain safety. We increased the number of safety audits, and set up coaching and individual psychological support for the ones who were leaving, but provided special coaching for the ones who were required until the final door was locked. One would expect that morale would be rock bottom, but although morale dipped initially, it picked up later and there was almost a trench mentality. Ironically, teamwork and productivity increased during the closure process, as during that period there was a sense of purpose. The site had been acquired in 1996, but unfortunately had to close in 2000 for tangible business reasons. The staff during that period had seen significant cultural and process change. It was never going to be easy integrating a regional family company into a large global organisation. The acquiring company, in this case DuPont, wanted to maintain the original company values of strong customer service and flexibility, while bringing its strong values of uniform operational business processes, ethics and safety. By and large, it worked, but it took effort, coaching and training. In this case, coaching meant regular one-to-one support and guidance from the new leaders sharing their experiences of the new ways of working, and the respective values. I remember the time clearly as there was uncertainty not only for me as a relatively new hire, but also for a large proportion of my staff who had never experienced a corporate culture before. I remember distinctly coaching my original staff on the benefits of a corporate culture, and what it could bring to them as individuals as well as the business. There was some understandable reticence, but I managed to keep the people we needed for the business, and nobody in my department left during that period. It was not an easy time during the four years – we experienced an unfortunate fatality, and intensive work preparing for a significant automotive quality certification. Even though a new, more corporate culture was implemented across the plant, it was executed in a caring way. It took some time, but this engendered trust. This was one of my significant personal learnings. It is noteworthy that the site closure was unforeseen at the time of acquisition. The caring approach made the redundancy process easier, not only because the severance packages were fair and reasonable, but also because the people had developed and were better prepared for the marketplace. Family organisations keep staff motivated through a sense of belonging and security, but not necessarily personal development beyond the basic business needs, or providing reasonable compensation and benefits for the lower echelons. These were the aspects I was trying to guide and coach the staff on at the time of the acquisition, with my knowledge of corporate culture. In the end, the maintenance staff left better skilled and better paid at the time of site closure.

I must say at the time when I was coaching staff I had not received any formal coach training. Business coaching was in its infancy at that time in the UK, and my practice was driven both by intuition, a requirement to drive results and knowing a different way of working was imperative.

We have seen that some of the eight characteristics are complementary, but they can also be at opposing ends of the spectrum. It is also worth noting that they are not necessarily mutually exclusive. Opposing subcultures may exist in large organisations that work together. The best way to look at this is in terms of values as well as culture. A company may have an overall culture based on its values, but still have subcultures at a site or departmental level driven by both respective maturity and business need. The IBM example demonstrates the existence of embedded company values. A research department developing a new product line would want to foster a sense of learning and enjoyment to support creativity, while still maintaining the need for results. An operational site making hazardous chemicals would need a sense of order, discipline and safety.

Groysberg et al. have done significant research with leaders and organisations to generate this, but, as always with these types of models, this is not an exact science and there is a level of interpretation. I use these models as useful guides to gain context and work plans or strategies, being mindful of the 80:20 rule. Hopefully, this has given me some insights into these cultural styles and how they can co-exist in large organisations if they are meeting the business outcomes. Cultures should not be transformed for their own sake, only if they need to be changed to deliver a desired outcome. Therefore, any leader needs to know where the organisation is at culturally before any changes are attempted. This can be done by assessment, survey, experience and intuition. This work should be the genesis of any change process.

I have discussed the power of coaching in the support of any change process, but not gone into any detail on coaching styles or processes. The styles and approaches will be determined by the coaches, as they have a library to choose from. However, depending on the cultural maturity, the overarching approach may be either transformational or transactional. There is a potential trap in the coaching profession, thinking that all coaching must be transformational, i.e. we are going to transform teams or people or processes, on the basis that there is perceived value only in the transformation process. However, coaching can be more transactional, i.e. guiding people from A to B in a process, rather than facilitating a transformation. The key elements are that any coaching process must ensure that it is not telling or consulting, and the client must own the outcome. This applies to teams as well as individuals. A coach will rely more on his/her personal experience as well as a coaching process but avoid either consulting or mentoring. In my experience, a more transactional approach is required when there is a specific business or team goal, and it is quite often used to support training, where individuals and teams need to move beyond knowledge towards implementation. There are plenty of instances where training is just not enough.

Throughout my consulting and operational career, I have delivered many workshops on safety and process improvement. These workshops require raising awareness and deep observation skills, but also a mindset shift. The first two can be delivered with functional training, but transformation is effected through coaching and role play. The latter requires one-to-one coaching. I always arrange coaching sessions and field observation to embed the learning. The mindset shift is about doing things differently. This is where coaching and training can work in a symbiotic way. A level of transaction is delivered, supported with transformation.

One approach for moving the behaviours and mindsets and to align expectations with the desired culture is to perform a 'From-To'-style visioning exercise after some level of analytics and cultural diagnoses, where we show the leaders what the current organisational behaviours are, based on confidential one-to-ones, focus groups and physical evidence as the 'From' state, and coach them through to what they want as the desired behaviours for the relevant culture. We will work with them to build a roadmap and action plan to deliver the change. I have successfully delivered these workshops in the areas of Capital Excellence (CAPEX), Operational Excellence (OPEX), Behavioural Safety and Process Safety. Where a leadership team is involved, coaches will be assigned to each of them. Generally, the cadence of the coaching is weekly or bi-monthly until the work is done. Sometimes the coaching is easier where the coach is there to support adherence to the action plan, and at other times the coach must draw on higher-end coaching skills. With the latter, it is usually because the leader has not fully bought into the changes, or they have a specific hurdle in terms of how to change. Quite often it is associated with workload too, as the leaders struggle to find time to deliver on the changes while still doing their day job. In this case, supplementary coaching can be delivered around empowerment and delegation.

The OCAI assessment

At this point I am going to discuss the OCAI (Organizational Culture Assessment Instrument) assessment and the work that supports it. I believe that it puts another interesting perspective on culture. I first came across it when I was researching materials for the change-management module for the MBA course. Essentially the team characterises four types of culture: Clan, Hierarchy, Adhocracy and Market (Figure 4.6). This is a four-point model that measures six characteristics of the organisation: dominant characteristics, organisational leadership, management of employees, organisational glue, strategic emphases and criteria for success. In Figure 4.6 you will see the culture types and the associated interactions and attributes of the cultures. There are competing or opposing values in the north–south and east–west axes again, with flexibility and freedom to act opposing stability and control, while external focus and differentiation oppose internal focus and integration. The originators describe these as values, but I see them more as attributes. They call it the 'Competing Values Framework'. It is possible to generate a plot in spider diagram format based on a questionnaire using 39 indicators. This gives you a 'heat map' of the organisational culture. It is very useful to get a sense check of

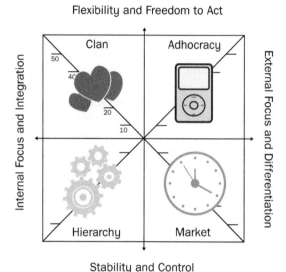

Figure 4.6   The OCAI competing values framework

where you are. The authors stress the benefits come from benchmarking and base-lining, prior to any company changes, what staff see as important, and a precursory insight to any mergers or reorganisations. The questionnaires are run in a way that you get an 'as-is' state and a 'preferred' state, so you get some insights into what the employee populations desire versus what they see that they have now. As with any questionnaires, these are the perceptions of the employees and not reality, so leaders need to bear this in mind when interpreting the data. The authors' descriptions of the four cultures are given below.

1. *Clan Culture.* A very pleasant place to work, where people share a lot of personal information, much like an extended family. The leaders or heads of the organisation are mentors and perhaps even parent figures. The organisation is held together by loyalty or tradition. Commitment is high. The organisation emphasises the long-term benefit of human resources development and attaches great importance to cohesion and morale. Success is defined in terms of sensitivity to customers and concern for people. The organisation places a premium on teamwork, participation and consensus.

2. *Adhocracy Culture.* A dynamic, entrepreneurial and creative place to work. People stick out their necks and take risks. The leaders are considered innovators and risk takers. The glue that holds the organisation together is commitment to experimentation and innovation. The emphasis is on being on the leading edge. The organisation's long-term emphasis is on growth and acquiring new resources. Success means gaining unique and new products or services. Being a product or service leader is important. The organisation encourages individual initiative and freedom.

3. *Market Culture*. A results-oriented organisation whose major concern is getting the job done. People are competitive and goal-oriented. The leaders are hard drivers, producers and competitors. They are tough and demanding. The glue that holds the organisation together is an emphasis on winning. Reputation and success are common concerns. The long-term focus is on competitive actions and achievement of measurable goals and targets. Success is defined in terms of market share and penetration. Competitive pricing and market leadership are important. The organisational style is hard-driving competitiveness.

4. *Hierarchy Culture*. A very formalised and structured place to work. Procedures govern what people do. The leaders pride themselves on being good coordinators and organisers who are efficiency-minded. Maintaining a smooth-running organisation is most critical. Formal rules and policies hold the organisation together. The long-term concern is stability and performance, with efficient, smooth operations. Success is defined in terms of dependable delivery, smooth scheduling and low cost. The management of employees is concerned with secure employment and predictability.

I asked the MBA students to run their own assessments as part of their course based on knowledge of their previous working experience. An analysis of these assessments was part of the essay question they had to complete to pass the module.

Although I was not aware of this model at the time, I have seen most of these cultures in both my operations and consulting careers. Generally, the cultures have been consistent in operations, mainly driven by the need for stability and control, and internal focus and integration. This is usually driven by the need to have standardisation within manufacturing. If you look at the model, then that would imply a hierarchical culture. But, as always, this is in degrees, and it is dependent on the age and maturity of the operation. Sometimes plant managers see themselves as 'benevolent dictators'. The idea is that they will get the place straight in line with business needs and incorporate best practice to get traction in the early days. Hence the attributes of internal focus and integration as they develop systems and processes and integrate functions. This is sometimes referred to as a directive culture. The workforce must put their faith in the plant manager and trust that they will get the help that they need and be looked after appropriately. There are times within operations that the Clan and Adhocracy cultures are beneficial in operations. A Clan culture can be useful in a time of stress where cohesion is required. Typically, this can be at times of product or line changes or where there are low volumes or pressure on productivity. I have seen elements of Adhocracy and Market cultures within operations, but that tends to be in smaller operational or family organisations where production, sales and R&D are in the same facility, and the business success is built on the symbiosis between these departments, where everyone helps everyone else and is expected to be a design and entrepreneurial element. For the sales function, they will of course be expected to be market-focused.

My consulting career has shown me that all cultures are prevalent. In consulting, you generally get involved in all aspects of work, from delivery and design to sales and business development. All of which require a strong market focus, creativity with dynamic solution design and control with respect to following internal processes. Large consulting firms have strong internal systems and devote considerable time to training their new hires in these to ensure a level of common understanding and consistency, which will not only give clients confidence, but will help with their brand equity. Knowing their markets, competitors and consequent strengths and weaknesses is also critical, as these days they are selling into a competitive market with more and more consultancies forming in the outsourced and gig economy. Even with the need for strong internal processes to provide consistent delivery, there will be a level of Adhocracy required to improvise in the field. No consultancy has a full understanding of the client culture before they go in to deliver, even though they may have a good idea of what to expect. To be effective, they must adapt to the client culture. I learned this early in my consulting career, while working in Russia. In Russia, generally they have a very distinct way of working, based on the need for detail and working within a hierarchy.

A more collegiate approach, which is what Western companies are used to, will not work initially. Consultancy engagements will inevitably require a level of cultural shift, and usually the promotion of greater teamwork, so here an approach that required shooting for the middle ground was agreed. Western companies are generally more collegiate and tend to be strategic, as well as driven by execution. That was our initial consulting approach with a top-down strategy, with high-level detail and then building more detail as the work progressed. The client was driven by a strong need for detail, almost a bottom-up approach. I referred earlier to the concept of postponed perfection, and the need for the 80:20 rule. We realised that after the first phase the gap was too wide for effective learning and knowledge transfer to take place. We grouped and realigned our teams to shoot for the middle ground, getting closer to the client's way of learning in our delivery approach, which was extremely successful. In the second phase we delivered considerably more value, and faster too. It also allowed us to standardise our future models for the future phases and clients in this region. I must stress at this point: this was the first time our Western consultants had ever delivered anything of this scale of complexity in Russia. Furthermore, we did do an adjustment in phase 1, when we recognised we were not delivering as well as we were capable of doing. We did engage a specialist external consultant to guide us on the correct approaches and cultural norms. This was my first exposure to the concept of 'intraculturality', back in 2011. This is based on the work of Geert Hofstede and his team, around the six cultural dimensions that can be prevalent in corporations, and that will vary in potency from region to region.

If I go back to my point about shooting for the middle ground when delivering knowledge and key messages through consulting and supported by coaching, then this is analogous to moving from push to pull. We need to 'pull' requirements from the client, and, when appropriate, 'push' knowledge. When I engage with consulting clients, whether corporates or smaller companies, I try to explain this at the start, so they have a good understanding of what to expect, and how the processes work. This also ties in with the need for authenticity and transparency. Clients always respond better when these explanations are made at the start. With coaching, it is worthwhile reiterating that coaching is always 'pull', because you are working to the client's agenda, and your role as a coach is to create a safe space where they can explore, share and move forward. The coach will be in active and intuitive listening mode. In a true coaching relationship, there should be no 'push' from the coach, just effective facilitation. It is also worthwhile exploring the current 'fear' and resistance to change. In most consulting engagements, the individuals you will be working with will not have been the decision-makers for the consulting engagement, so there will be a level of reticence, fear and potential resistance. Therefore, I always share the process and expectations upfront with each client representative.

Hofstede and intraculturality

The final cultural element in this chapter is that of 'intraculturality'. This is the work pioneered by Geert Hofstede and his Institute. The main tenet of his work is understanding how cultures vary, even in the same functions and departments, in large corporations, and from region to region. That is, regions can have specific cultures and identities. This is a critical understanding for large corporations, because this can impact the way that they perform in different regions, when deciding which approaches are required to sustain and develop a business, or even move into a new region. Traditionally companies have acquired this knowledge based on a combination of experience, local independent knowledge, a path-finding approach, or even intuition. The Hofstede Institute has brought a more rigorous approach, and some behavioural science. This not only enhances predictability, results, common understanding and faster results, but also fosters greater teamwork and engagement. As I mentioned earlier, I first came across this work in Russia. We were dealing with a more hierarchical culture than expected. Figure 4.2 on p. 33 presents a simple assessment to illustrate consultancy challenges around getting workforces to be less risk averse. It is possible do simple assessments online that will give you a flavour, without signing up for detailed assessments.

Hofstede's six cultural dimensions are described as Power Distance, Individualism, Masculinity, Uncertainty Avoidance, Long-Term Orientation and Indulgence. These cultural dimensions are all elements of a culture in a region, and countries and regions can be compared against one another relatively. Not every country has a data set for each dimension. In Figure 4.2, data is missing for both Long-Term Orientation and Indulgence for Qatar. It will take quite some work to complete these, as one would imagine. These illustrations act as a ready reckoner to help you get a flavour of the country or region. The definitions are as follows:

1. Power Distance relates to the different solutions to the basic problem of human inequality.
2. Uncertainty Avoidance relates to the level of stress in a society in the face of an unknown future.
3. Individualism versus Collectivism relates to the integration of individuals into primary groups.

4. Masculinity versus Femininity relates to the division of emotional roles between women and men.
5. Long-Term versus Short-Term Orientation relates to the choice of focus for people's efforts: the future or the present and past.
6. Indulgence versus Restraint relates to the gratification versus control of basic human desires related to enjoying life.

It is possible to go deeper by purchasing a more in-depth survey, or engaging with one of the Hofstede Institute's associate consultants, who will work with your organisation to assess the current regional cultural dimensions and prepare action plans to move forward. The major point of this model is that it is cross-border. Executing an analysis like this will help leadership teams and change agents identify either the barriers or enablers for improvement or change when moving into an area or region, or making significant change in an area. All of these are important to a corporate culture, but in my experience dimensions 1, 2, 3 and 5 have the most relevance. I have seen Power Distance be most prevalent in my engagements in Russia and Qatar. These have the potential to act as barriers, because they can inhibit team engagement and true empowerment. A strong Power Distance can manifest itself in many ways. I have seen it where execution teams are inhibited from making decisions, without referral to a senior leader. In the most extreme cases, I have seen decisions reversed the following day by a supervisor. This culture can trigger secondary challenges around micro-management. When we were in the first phase in Russia, I recall our team having to account for the day while consulting virtually every 15 minutes when working with the client team, while we planned to split it into quarter days. This was not because we had to justify our value, but because they had to explain their time to their supervisors. In one extreme case, I had planned a one-day workshop for two days to allow for translation. I finished it in one and a half days, which in a Western, more collegiate culture, would have been considered a success. I received great feedback on content and delivery. However, the following day, I was quizzed by the team, because they were unable to justify finishing half a day earlier to their bosses. In a less hierarchical and more collegiate culture, they would have been glad for the extra time they had gained. In these cultures, they must justify every minute, and have little freedom to operate. Quite often in these cultures, their working lives are dominated by fear. I will discuss fear and value in a coaching context later in the book.

The second dimension, Uncertainty Avoidance, is currently very relevant because of global geopolitics, which is creating a very uncertain situation. I also refer to the VUCA business environment I mentioned in Chapter 1. This will exacerbate the situation, but some cultures and regions are more prone to Uncertainty Avoidance. If we refer to Figure 4.2, we see that Russia has a very high Uncertainty Avoidance, which may be a throwback to the old Soviet regime. This was obvious in my consulting engagement in Russia.

Then, if we take the Individualism versus Collectivism dimension, this is important when building or integrating teams. Those areas that have low levels of Individualism and consequently high levels of Collectivism, are more likely to embrace new people and have a sense of shared responsibility. If we refer to Figure 4.2, we will see that the United States has a high score for Individualism, which is consistent with what I have seen in both consulting and operations. When we review these dimensions, we need to ensure that we do not fall into the trap of assuming that one is better than the other. One might assume that, for large corporations, Collectivism is better, but individuals lead teams, and furthermore sometimes you need to have people 'break out'. In extreme cases of Collectivism, I have seen talented individuals dragged down by the group.

I am not going to spend too long discussing the fifth dimension of Long-Term versus Short-Term Orientation, but clearly having a longer-term view will help with sustainable cultural transformation if applied correctly.

At this point, we have discussed and explored various types of organisational cultures, at least 12: eight from one model and four for another. Furthermore, we have also looked at the impact of regional cultures. There are also specific cultures that are necessary to support a business, not just drive it. A good example is that of a process safety culture which is necessary for the chemicals and petrochemicals industries, and that of ethics for banking, finance and many others. These are rightly now part of the boardroom agenda. There are many others that fit in with the 12 types mentioned in this chapter.

We have seen the various attributes and characteristics of each, how they intersect and interact. There was an overlap between the characteristics of the elements in each model, which is inevitable. Certain departments and functions are more prone to exhibit specific characteristics of the cultures. There is no hard-and-fast approach for coaching these to effect appropriate change or cultural shift. If you are going to have a sustainable change, it is just as important to know your starting point as knowing where you plan to end up culturally. The starting point will give you a view of the challenges ahead. An assessment using these models will give you a rough idea of the starting point. The visioning work you do with your teams will help you with the end. As a leader, you can then start to build a roadmap between the two. As mentioned before, this type of work is not an exact science. The roadmap you build will reflect the business needs and the challenges. The roadmap should be designed and built by the leadership team. If it is a two- to five-year programme, the milestones will probably change slightly, but that won't matter if the predicted outcomes at each stage are reasonably close to the plan, and the direction of travel is consistent with the planned course. Therefore, a strategic plan is essential and regular team check-ins between the key milestones are important. I am working with a consulting team now where the client requires a significant move towards an improved process safety performance. As would be expected, there are attributes associated with a poor safety culture, such as low accountability, poor attention to detail, low risk perception, poor communication, lack of follow-up, and many others. An early diagnostic is essential. It is only when you get truly embedded in the organisation that you truly understand what it really is. Hence the need for regular check-ins or recalibrations. As the lead coach and responsible person for mindsets and behaviours, I have just initiated this. The negative aspects of the poor safety culture were much worse than we expected. We are going to deliver more coaching resource and alter the scope accordingly to meet the deeper challenges.

Some of our coaching activities will change in a way that will drive accountability more. Frequency of field assessments will increase. However, it is important not to overwhelm people, so these have been simplified. When making significant changes, it is important to stay tuned to individual client and team energy levels to avoid burnout. Simple confidential pulse-style surveys can help here.

Another key learning is to make sure that you are realistic at the start with your planned outcomes and achievements, particularly regarding timing. I have seen many programmes where the timing is far too ambitious. Any check-in process requires absolute openness and transparency, not just with the client, but within the delivery team. This is another reason why consultant and coaching team selection is critical, not only from a functional skills perspective, but also from a workability and a mutual respect perspective. In the article 'Tipping point leadership',[13] Kim and Mauborgne describe how former New York City Police Commissioner Bill Bratton built his change team, made them more accountable, fostered absolute transparency and put the resources where he needed them most to sort out New York's crime problems. Large challenges require a focused and dynamic response, especially when there are embedded cultural norms that need to be changed. The problems that Bill Bratton faced are analogous to those faced in my current assignment. Furthermore, the coaching style has to adapt in a way that helps drive more accountability. If you are going to facilitate more accountability, you must build more trust. The two go hand in hand. It is a simple two-way agreement for the coach and client: you help them to deliver more, so you must give more. These elements must always be in balance. I have seen plenty of situations where coaching processes have gone awry, because the balance gets upset, and the process becomes too transactional or directive. A highly trained coach will always stay self-aware and mindful of the client's needs so this does not happen. Professionally trained coaches will always be curiously mindful and be coached themselves.

A few final reflections on coaching in large organisations that are looking to shift cultures and affect change. It is important that the coaching process stays appropriate and does not become transactional or merely a tick-box process, especially if these sessions will usually cover a period of up to two years or beyond. It is important to build trust and get the chemistry right between coaches and clients. Sometimes it is important to match coach seniority with status in the client organisation, but in theory this should not matter. It depends on the type of organisation; this is more prevalent in a hierarchical status-driven organisation. If the chemistry is wrong, switch people around as soon as possible. A strong coach will never worry about the breakdown of a coaching relationship, unless they know they have done something wrong, in which case this will be a learning opportunity. A strong coach training programme will ensure that a coach is adequately trained to deal with this situation. Coaching is a dynamic process, which is why it is so suited to facilitating cultural change. Coaches are change leaders and, when working together with clients, form a powerful alliance that not only effects change, but can understand cultural and team dynamics, which is essential to keep a programme on track. They quite often see things that others don't, due to their training and deep awareness.

Synthesis

Finally, I refer to Figure 4.7, a model which I have developed to help people visualise cultural transformation. Every cultural transformation process requires three key elements or specific changes. First, improved systems and processes, which are the transactional or consulting piece of work. Second, we need a behavioural shift in the staff, which is where coaching supports. Finally, a passion for change in individuals, the team and the organisation. This one is often forgotten and potentially is the most important and one of the key reasons change programmes fail. Passion will drive the programme sustainability. I liken the model to a three-legged stool. If you remove one of the legs, it will fall over. I will be referring to this model later in the book, because I find it powerful as an illustration as we go on the change journey. A simple question to ask: are we delivering on all three elements? The model illustrates why coaching and consultancy can work in harmony to deliver change. When setting up a coaching programme and/or consulting programme for change with a team, be clear on roles and responsibilities within the team and even consider a RACI diagram (see Figure 2.3 on p. 10). Watch out for overlaps and gaps. The overlaps are less obvious than the gaps and can cause stress within the client team, especially if one member is consulting a client staff member for the purposes of knowledge transfer, and another is coaching them. I reiterate, coaching and consulting are different, and when they are confused, problems usually ensue.

Cultural transformation differs from change management in that it should be sustainable, and, if effected properly, self-sustaining in that a business can keep evolving. As Richard Edelmen explains 'Engagement and integrity are the two most fundamental aspects of building trust; lead from the front by evolving your company strategy, then live your values every day.'[14]

Cultural indicators, surveys and interviews

Before I reflect on this chapter, let us touch on how coaches and coach leaders can get a feel for the culture of the organisations they are in if they are internal coaches,

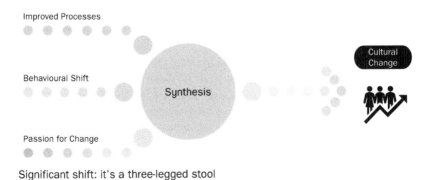

Significant shift: it's a three-legged stool

Figure 4.7 Cultural transformation synthesis model

or will be working with external coaches. I will be covering hostile cultures in Chapter 6. As an internal coach, you will have an inkling of what the organisation style is, based on the style of management interactions, communications, leadership behaviours and other factors. Some companies like employee surveys, but there are downsides to this. Some people believe that surveys can be useful in providing a cultural baseline. Having delivered a few, I think the key advantage of a survey is that it can trigger an effective dialogue by asking searching questions. Given our discussion on intraculturality, this should be factored into any survey, as the answers can be skewed. Basic surveys can give some indication, but do not over-interpret the data. More sophisticated surveys can be used, especially if you have behavioural scientists on the HR or Marketing teams, as some larger companies do. There are some well-thought-out approaches to doing surveys. In their *Harvard Business Review* article, Scott Judd, Eric O'Rourke and Adam Grant state that surveys are one of the best ways to measure employee engagement.[15] Employee engagement is a great indicator of the type of company culture. It will not give you all the answers, but it is a good place to start. A word of caution on surveys: as I mentioned earlier, it is prudent to get the professionals involved where you can, such that the survey can be structured appropriately. I know from bitter experience that a badly designed survey can do more harm than good. Explaining poor surveys can suck up time and energy, and lose credibility for the PM team and leaders. I have used an article by Morrel-Samuels recently as a framework for co-designing a recent survey.[16] It gives good guidance on the strengths and pitfalls. All surveys take time and diligence.

I find interviewing the leadership team a very powerful way of understanding the culture. Over the years, I have designed a set of questions for the leadership team, and these are usually done within the first week of the process. The questions have a core theme and framework, and are tailored to both the function and the leadership level. For large engagements, I ask for a diagonal slice of the organisation, so we get a cross-section of function and level in a matrix. The questions must be relevant to the roles, but time should not be wasted in over-design. For a large corporate client, with multiple sites, I would group the levels thus:

- Senior Leader, VP, C-Suite
- Director, Site Manager
- Unit Manager, Functional Leader
- Line Leader or Supervisor.

For a manufacturing organisation, I would talk to levels across production, engineering, maintenance, logistics and possibly research. For a marketing organisation, I would talk to marketing, sales, communications, advertising and creative functions. The aim is the same across any organisation and that is to build an initial picture of its structure. We will also delve deeper to get worker feedback, as this is a good test. The same principles apply, but the nature of how this is executed depends on the size and type of organisation. So the themes usually covered are listed below. As mentioned earlier, the questions are tailored to the individuals.

Typical question themes are:

- engagement and connection with other levels (communication)
- ability to 'walk the talk' (role-modelling behaviour)
- time spent away from the desk
- meeting effectiveness
- self-development
- people development
- response to difficult situations/times
- personal integrity, authenticity, congruence.

The questions are always asked in a descriptive way and in a non-confrontational tone, as in when, how, what, where? It is critical to preserve anonymity in any feedback, and that is also made clear at the start of any session. A typical question could be, 'When was the last time you went on the shop floor and what did you do?' The trick is to leave the questions short and open and let the client 'do the talking'. I never ask all the questions, and let the conversation flow. The more senior the person, the shorter the list.

Leadership interview feedback should be combined with survey feedback and 'focus groups' if you are able to do them. Focus groups are a great way of getting feedback and understanding the energy of the organisation. When designing group sessions, you need to consider the cultural hierarchy in the organisation, i.e. if there is strong Power Distance, there is no point in putting different managerial levels together as they will not speak up. It is also useful to mix functions, however if there is open or implicit hostility between groups, then do not do so. The aim is to get people to talk freely.

This will give a flavour of how to understand the culture of an organisation. There are no hard-and-fast rules and a coach will get better at this the more they do it. I have led numerous cultural diagnostics in large organisations, and when we come to synthesise the data, it is a rewarding and powerful process. Even though these can be qualitative rather than quantitative results, they are amazingly accurate. The key point is that everything needs to be evidence-based. You are looking for information as much as data. This is your opportunity to go deeper. I always run a post-diagnostic validation process. The earlier you start this process, the more productive it will be, with less waste.

Key takeaways

- Two of the most powerful levers available to leaders to improve the strength of the business are strategy and culture. Strategy needs to be dynamic to meet the demands of the new VUCA world and the dynamic element needs to be part of the ongoing cultural development. Having the correct culture for an organisation is critical to its ongoing success. Even if the culture is embedded, it can be developed through coaching and change programmes to meet the needs of the business.

- A cultural transformation occurs when the way people work together and solve problems changes. Cultural transformation differs from change management in that is sustainable and self-supporting. A change management programme can be discrete.
- Specific industry subcultures run across different companies in the same industries.
- Irrespective of the business sector, companies that have a strong values base can generally react well to varying market conditions and fluctuations. This makes coaching easier. It is not about shifting values but using the significant core of the values to develop the people and the business.
- Regional cultural norms do exist and can have a massive impact on how you approach a cultural change programme. This is exemplified in the work of Geert Hofstede and his six cultural dimensions.
- There are various definitions of company or organisational culture, and understanding them is important, i.e. knowing your start point is critical to developing the culture the business needs. The most successful leaders know where they are before they embark on change.
- The characteristics of coaches and strong leaders are similar. They need to be a bit radical, transformational and, most importantly, take personal risk by exposing themselves and their thinking.
- Trust and authenticity are critical to great coaching. Trust must be gained at the start and maintained. There are well-founded ways of delivering this based on coaching practice and training.
- Some level of resistance to change is inevitable but knowing the phases and how to react from a coaching and a leadership perspective will increase the chances of success. Remember the resistance that Bill Bratton experienced in the Kim and Mauborgne article, and know that the source of resistance is not always obvious.
- Staff reactions to culture change are not always as would be expected. Even in times of great stress, staff can react in a positive way almost beyond survival and into interdependence.
- Coaching for cultural transformation is a dynamic process, which is built on awareness and chemistry.
- Great leaders and coaches see things that others do not.
- Do the cultural diagnostic early in any transformation process and get information from multiple sources. Information validation and anonymity are the key to a successful diagnostic.

5   Change management models: Description and facets

Established models

In this chapter I will describe some well-known change models, appraise their relative benefits, and see how coaching fits in with these models. As with the cultural attributes and characteristics, there will inevitably be some cross-over between the models. I will start with the definitions of 'change management'. Before we look at the concept of change management, we need to go back to basics, and understand what 'change' is. As an engineer, I like things simple and clear, so the definition that resonates is, 'the process or result of becoming different'. Numerous change management programmes in business have failed for a variety of reasons. Therefore, it is critical that any organisation, before embarking on a programme, must have a clear vision and outcomes, i.e. there must be a notable and noticeable difference. I will make a connection between individual coaching and change management. Both require a shift in outcomes. Marshall Goldsmith, in his book *What Got You Here Won't Get You There*,[1] talks about the importance of announcing any shift in behaviour, as otherwise it can go unnoticed by peers; particularly in the case of small changes, peers, associates or family will naturally assume nothing has changed, even if it possibly has. With a programme, the staff must see the change and live it, otherwise it will not be sustainable.

If we go deeper into the definitions, change management (sometimes abbreviated as CM) is a collective term for all approaches to preparing and supporting *individuals, teams* and *organisations* in making *organisational change*. It includes methods that redirect or redefine the use of resources, business process, budget allocations or other modes of operation that significantly change a company or organisation. Organisational change management (OCM) considers the full organisation and what needs to change, while change management may be used solely to refer to how people and teams are affected by such organisational transition. It deals with many different disciplines, from behavioural and social sciences to information technology and business solutions.

Definitions of change management are as diverse as the challenges clients may be facing, given today's ever evolving business environment characterised by rapid rates of change, uncertainty and complexity. Change management is a systemic approach and the application of '[knowledge,] tools and resources to leverage the benefits of change, managing an as-is process or function, moving towards a better or more efficient process or function in hopes positively to impact performance'.[2] To achieve this, change must be effective, successful and, most importantly, sustainable. Change management entails thoughtful planning, sensitive implementation and consultation with, and involvement of, the people affected by a specific change. Increasingly, change management is seen as a permanent business function to improve productivity and profits by keeping organisations adaptable to the competitive marketplace. Change must be realistic, achievable and measurable.

It makes sense to start with Kurt Lewin, as his was an early model of change. Kurt Lewin published his model as long ago as 1958.[3] He proposed his three-stage model of unfreezing, changing and refreezing. On the surface, it is a very simple approach and can be explained in the following way. The first stage is the need to unfreeze or thaw the attributes that have been embedded in an organisation. The second stage is to make the requisite changes and, finally, freeze the new attributes or ways of working. The advantage of this model is that it has total clarity, meaning that it is easily understood, not only by those who will effect the changes, but also by the whole organisation. However, although it has the upside of clarity and simplicity, its downside is that it does not have clear stages for execution, i.e. it is not very transactional. I see this model more as a philosophy or a way of thinking, to understand the prerequisites for effective change. Furthermore, from an execution perspective, it is easy to see how difficult it can be to define clear boundaries for the three stages, and it is possible to get stuck. With the other models discussed later, the stages have greater definition, and there are more of them. If we look at this end to end, one could argue that this three-stage model would overlap with, say, Kotter's 8-step model. Thus, there would be multiple elements of Kotter's model covered by the three stages of Lewin's. Lewin did get people thinking about change, and the need for some level of structure and understanding. When I am guiding and coaching leaders through a change management process, I use the Lewin model as a means of illustrating the macro model for change. Furthermore, Lewin was able to highlight the difficulty of making significant change in any organisation. Arguably stage 2 is the easiest, because it is more transactional. Unfreezing at stage 1 will require a significant mindset shift and, given my coaching experience, I know this is not easy, either as an organisation or for individuals. I refer to my previous observations on company and regional cultures. Quite often stage 3 never actually happens because leaders and teams have a tendency to stop short of embedding the new culture or work practices. Given that change is difficult, leaders, managers and team members can give a collective sigh of relief before the new ways of working are properly solidified or embedded.

At this point, it is worthwhile talking about the influence of coaching on change. Coaching is just one element of a change management programme, and its primary purpose is to support teams on their team and individual journeys. It is not there to transfer knowledge or 'upskill' directly.

I regularly work on change management programmes where clients want to make changes to the way they work to obtain better results that support an improved business outcome. There are many different programmes; the ones I am most involved with are 'Process Safety', 'Capital Effectiveness' and 'Operational Excellence'. Although these have different business outcomes, the core of each is similar. Furthermore, an effective coaching programme to support these is essential.

I mentioned earlier that the 'unfreezing' process can be the most difficult as it requires a shift in mindset, and the consequent behaviour that goes with it. The training usually is split into two categories. These are soft skills, where individuals and teams are taught new ways of behaving, and functional training where they are taught functional skills, such as problem solving, cost estimation, basic statistics, and others. The soft skills workshops are critical in supporting the coaching effort. The topics covered in these workshops include giving and receiving feedback and having difficult conversations. These raise the levels of awareness that are required for those who are on the change journey and provide the opportunity for reflective learning. The coaching comes in where teams or individuals have problems dealing with specific issues. This is exactly where the coaching supports the change process. Figure 5.1 shows the coaching elements and relationships model, but not everyone buys into the change immediately, even if they know they must. Many of my clients, whether part of a corporate or business programme, struggle with change and get stuck in the earlier phases of the model. These struggles can involve dealing with other team members, process changes, workload, different ways of working and many others. Humans are creatures of a habit and change is unnatural. Coaching is

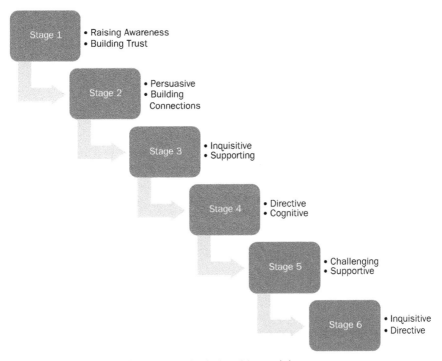

Figure 5.1 Coaching elements and relationship model

a process that lets people deal with the change around them and execute change themselves. It can take numerous sessions and different approaches to get there, but virtually all those who want change will get there. It is immensely rewarding for the client, as they have made a great achievement themselves. In my experience, this sense of achievement generates momentum and the potential for further success. One of the reasons, I have related the coaching process to this model is to illustrate in a clear way the synergy between coaching, training and the context of change. We will come back to the role of coaching with the other models.

Model comparisons

Jick's 10-stage model

Professor Todd Jick designed his 10-stage management model for tactical change in the early 1990s.[4] His model is very much based on 'how' to implement change and bears some similarity to Kotter's 8-step model, albeit with additional steps and different emphases and order in a couple of places.

These are the 10 simple steps (the Jick model):

1. Analyse the organisation and the need for change.
2. Create a shared vision and common direction.
3. Separate from the past.
4. Create a sense of urgency.
5. Support a strong leader role.
6. Line up political sponsorship.
7. Craft and implement a plan.
8. Develop enabling structures.
9. Communicate, involve people and be honest.
10. Reinforce and institutionalise the change.

The two models have the same approach, although with its additional stages the Jick model is more comprehensive. The beauty of these models lies in their logical steps, and the staged development is like the original Lewin model in that it aims to take the leaders and teams who are involved on a journey to the end point.

Kotter's 8-step model

Kotter's 8-step model (1996)[5] is based on the work of Kurt Lewin. Kotter's steps are as follows:

1. Create a sense of urgency.
2. Build a guiding coalition.
3. Develop a vision and strategy.

4. Communicate the change vision.
5. Empower broad-based action.
6. Generate short-term wins.
7. Consolidate gains and produce more change.
8. Anchor new approaches in the culture.

There is probably more context in the Jick model in that it refers to honesty in stage 9. Honesty and authenticity are fundamental building blocks for any change process, and at the core of any programme. Overall, you will only observe subtle differences in the two models, but the key point here is that both share the same end which is about embedding the new ways of working in the new culture. I have used the key elements of the Kotter model in my consulting work. I find it simpler for most clients to understand as there is a clear logical flow. Step 6 of the Kotter model is also critical as it ties in very much with a 'lean' approach, and the thinking of the 80:20 rule and generating traction. Generating short-term wins is critical for success.

In my current engagement we are running monthly campaigns as part of the transformation process so that the shop floor personnel can see simple visible change as a means of engagement. I have worked with some very tough clients, where because the staff had been accustomed to hearing the same promised change rhetoric, they would no longer believe that tangible, constructive and sustainable change would ever happen. These are exactly the situations where you need quick wins. I have an associate who has had a strong and successful career in sales, who guided me to imagine everyone in the audience I was pitching to for a consultancy job had a Post-It® note on their foreheads saying, 'So what?' I carry that forward to any coaching or consulting delivery where I am responsible for communicating change. This is a good reminder to be focused on the quick wins. The Kotter model tends also to be more widely published and used. There are plenty of online videos of him explaining the concepts, which helps when you are getting the message across.

One final reflection on these two models is that the Jick model does refer to lining up the political sponsorship with step 6. There is some potential overlap with Kotter's step 6, but this is more explicitly about dealing with stakeholders, even potentially difficult ones, which is very important and often forgotten. I have previously mentioned the 60:20:20 model (see Figure 4.4) and this applies to key stakeholders as well as general staff. Sorting out the political and potential detractors is critical for success. This was one of the key success factors for Bill Bratton when he was sorting out the issues with the NYPD. My only criticism of this element is that it comes too late and should be earlier than step 6 for all the reasons mentioned. Stakeholder management is critical in any consultancy delivery.

The ADKAR® model

I will now move on to the fourth and final model: the ADKAR® model. The ADKAR® model was developed by Jeff Hiatt in 2003. It is one of the more recent and well-understood change management models. ADKAR® is an acronym for:

- *A*wareness (Employees must be made aware of the need for change.)
- *D*esire (Employees must have the desire to participate and fully support the change.)
- *K*nowledge (By gathering knowledge about the change process, the (ultimate) goal of the change will become clear for the employees.)
- *A*bility (Because of the ability to learn new skills and by managing behaviour, change is accepted.)
- *R*einforcement (Reinforcement to sustain the change makes it clear to all employees that there is no turning back,)

As mentioned, change management is usually met with employee resistance. The model was specifically designed this way and offers a clear level of understanding and simplicity. The model was subsequently introduced by PROSCI®, a change management consultancy, as a practical tool. Formal training and workbooks on ADKAR® are available to support the model. Another key element of the design was to help employees through the process. This is a licensed product[6] and therefore I have not delivered it or come across it directly. However, I considered it beneficial to cover it here, due to several of its benefits such as its simplicity and the clarity of understanding at all levels of the organisation, which fosters engagement. I have done my own research on the model, and interviewed an associate, Ursula Wandrag, who has been formally PROSCI®-trained and has delivered the model in a consultancy environment. I have detailed her experiences and observations below and added my own thoughts from a coaching perspective.

> ### Pros and cons of the ADKAR® model

Based on my own experience of Energy Leadership coaching, acronyms and the basis of a common language aid learning, engagement and embedding the concepts. Although the ADKAR® model has fewer steps than the other models, you will again see some overlap and the fact it takes staff on a journey, whereby there is a raising of awareness, and a conclusion with reinforcement of the change, akin to Lewin's refreezing. There is a lot more emphasis on employee understanding with this model, and you can tell this by the language used for the stages. The words used are more people-centred and empathetic, particularly regarding awareness, desire, knowledge and ability. These give a more transformational feel. One could surmise that reinforcement is more transactional.

In my discussions with Ursula, she revealed that the model is easy to explain, which allows people to start using it early. Furthermore, the common language in the model enables staff to talk more easily about tough subjects. The model is empowering and allows managers and supervisors to identify and discuss areas where staff are getting stuck or have personal roadblocks. There is a very strong parallel here with the techniques we use to ease energy blockers in coaching. Ursula confirmed that the process, training, workbooks and e-learning modules help leaders help staff approach these issues. As always with any business approach, however, the model has its detractors. There are also practical ways of measuring morale or resistance to change, and whether staff are moving along the change journey. I have found some ways of measuring positive morale or resistance to change. If we take morale first, then we can look at simple metrics such as the number of positive interventions or formal and informal recognition of staff peer-to-peer. This can be very powerful, but it is important it does not become trite or self-serving. There are other ways, such as the ability to give feedback without the fear of retribution. Finally, the ability to have a 'difficult conversation' is important. I will often give training on this, along with giving and receiving feedback to help the process. There is also recognition of a higher-functioning culture, and higher levels of staff engagement.

We can now look at some detractors or lagging indicators, which have a strong link to resistance to change. There are many, but I will pick out a few, based on experience. These should be obvious to most, but poor attendance at meetings, ineffective meetings and lack of focus can all be negative indicators. There are two ways to mitigate this. If there is a general malaise, training on meeting effectiveness can help. If it is one or two individuals, then the coaching programme can be intensified for them. In situations of low morale, or resistance to change, early recognition and intervention are critical. ADKAR® generally works well in business cultures where openness and honesty are core values. The ADKAR® mindset works best alongside the PROSCI® methodology.

This emphasises the need to select carefully which change management model is selected at the start. It is critical to consider the desired outcomes, do research and take guidance before selecting the appropriate model.

One final reflection on the models: when selecting a model, go beyond the desired outcomes, and consider buy-in from staff, potential resistance to change and ease of implementation. One other factor to consider is that in certain countries and cultures, the process of change and implementation can easily be confused. This is a common error, and I have witnessed this both personally and anecdotally from associates. For the purposes of clarity, implementation is the process of executing the desired outcomes required at each step of the change process, and change is the visible or tangible shift that a company and staff makes in its everyday work.

My coaching experience and change models

We have seen some comparison of the models, but how about the coaching techniques? There are numerous coaching systems, far too many to cover them all. All have sets of tools or approaches, and some of these are common to different systems. I have mentioned before that I have been formally trained in both NLP and Energy Leadership. These systems can be used in all walks of life and situations. Situations can range from life coaching, leadership coaching and team coaching, to executive coaching, group coaching and team coaching. There are a couple more systems worthy of mention which are somatic and embodiment coaching. These are part of a new way of thinking, which covers both body and mind. Somatic coaching is a holistic approach. The word 'somatics' comes from the Greek root *soma*, which means 'the living body in its wholeness'. This coaching is a way to view or observe people holistically. It is a process in which one embodies new practices in a way that creates a body of action. It is a different coaching style that brings the whole body to the fore, as an advocate in creating a place for personal transformation. Conceptually, our bodies are constructed through our personal lifetime and are a function of how we are raised, and our relationships with our friends, peers and associates.

I have not really experienced somatic coaching in a business environment but know that some companies offer workshops and meditation sessions. This type of approach is not for everyone, and we must remember that the coaching programmes are not there in their own right, but to support a business change process. As we become more emotionally aware, I can see that somatic coaching will increase its bandwidth.

I will refer to the two systems I have been trained in. I first trained in NLP back in 2008, and still use some of the approaches. As with all forms of coaching, the specific approach should reflect the client's need. The basic tenet of NLP is that it is a communication system. It is considered the representation of the experience of how people communicate with themselves and others. The origins go back to Richard Bandler and John Grinder in the 1970s.[7] There are numerous papers and scholarly articles on NLP, and the British Psychological Society is a rich source of information. It is important to note that although NLP has some roots in psychology, it is not all about psychology which can put some people off as they consider it to be potentially manipulative. If you research NLP, you will see a very comprehensive suite of approaches, which includes elements such as the Wheel of Life, the Leadership Style Questionnaire, Emotional Intelligence Assessment, the Personal Direction Tool, Anchoring, Metaphors, the Circle of Excellence, and Delegating Negative Self-Talk. Even though my most recent coach training experience is Energy Leadership (EL), I use these approaches in varying situations. Most of the above tools are common to EL. The tools can be used in a group or team environment, but generally work best for individuals, as these approaches are personal.

I first came across Energy Leadership coaching when I was doing the research for my diploma in 2013. Other systems were available, but they had a greater overlap with NLP, and I was looking to stretch myself and learn more. I would advise anybody who is considering professional coaching as a vocation, to ask some critical and fundamental questions such as the following. Am I open-minded? Am I curious? Am I focused on personal growth? Furthermore, what I found useful was my previous training in lean, as this is grounded in the belief of 'continuous improvement'. As it turned out, the iPEC (Institute for Professional Excellence in Coaching) had a comprehensive evaluation process for admissions. This process is very helpful for doing your 'inner work' and self-reflection in a way that ensures you feel you meet the criteria. The EL programme had some other advantages. Like other coaching programmes, it is based on the principles of being non-judgemental. This is critical if you are going to have an impactful relationship with a client. Although I did not know the specific details, my logical brain understood the principle that personal performance is linked to energy. Our energy can be shifted with coaching techniques to improve our performance. I also liked the idea that it was possible to do a well-structured assessment of an individual's resonating energy, which was not related to either skills, experience or personality. I knew from my previous work experience that an assessment was a great precursor to a strong coaching dialogue. Even if the situation is not right for delivering an ELI assessment, just discussing the concepts of Energy Leadership can significantly raise the self-awareness of clients who wish to improve their leadership skills, even in consulting environments. EL ticked all the boxes for me, so I embarked on the programme, which was a great experience, not only from a learning perspective but also from a relationship-building perspective. I am still in regular contact with the alumni community and a significant proportion of my cohort. A shared experience builds bonds, which is another critical element of any cultural transformation or change management programme.

I learned that there are many influences on our personal energy levels, but I found the most critical ones for development and activating effective change are levels of self-awareness and the environment. Here we do not just mean the physical environment, but the culture or working environment. Once a client knows that if they have a positive influence on their working environment they can shift their average energy, this is a really uplifting experience for them. So how can they change or influence their environment? This can be through having team meetings, discussions or dialogues in an open way, which may challenge a culture of fear or oppression. At this point, it is worth discussing the influence of self-awareness. Self-awareness can improve personal energy. Generally, this is where the coach helps the client with what we call 'inner work' or self-reflection. This is yet another bonus of understanding the concept of Energy Leadership. Self-awareness not only improves our energy but can help us improve our working environment in a symbiotic way. This approach is extremely powerful even in the most challenging of situations.

I am currently coaching a leader as part of a significant consulting engagement and part of a three-year change management programme. He is buried in a mountain of work and overwhelmed. He understands that the programme is essential for the business to be more productive and to be less variable. He has excellent technical and functional skills but is struggling to engage with his team in an effective way. I know how it feels to be in this situation. The team have not explicitly said anything about the leadership style, but it is obvious from their body language and some of the subliminal messages and behaviour in meetings. Some coaches would advocate a 360 survey by his peers, reports and leaders. I have clearly stated this is not required. If there are leadership and communication issues, what benefit would a 360 bring? In fact, some believe that 360 surveys can be damaging, because they are formed from a perspective that there is an 'issue', and can be judgemental or negative. A 2011 *Harvard Business Review* article by Marcus Buckingham[8] described the potential negative impacts of a 360, based on the fact it starts by assuming a relative position, i.e. better than or worse, rather than an absolute position. This, by its very nature, can create an aura of judgement. An effective coaching dialogue on the importance of self-awareness proved to be very effective, without the potential for judgement. Maintaining an environment of non-judgement also ensures that energy is not negatively impacted. In the end, the client raised his self-awareness, and improved his communication and leadership style. This also improved the working environment, not only for him, but also for his team and peers.

This approach is not just powerful on its own, but as an enabler for other leadership improvements, such as empowerment and delegation. These are critical leadership skills but tend to be more transactional in nature. I often deliver workshops on empowerment and delegation as part of consulting. I avoid delivering these types of workshops until I have met the teams, and observed them in meetings and individually, and understand the team dynamics. If necessary, I will do individual or team coaching and a workshop on self-awareness and the importance of building trust first. Trust building and self-awareness are also key enablers for so many other aspects of the coaching relationship. This leads on to another coaching skill: the power of observation. To deliver productive workshops as described above and execute coaching, it is fundamental to be able to observe effectively. Those who are trainers will know this, as it is critical to be able to read the room when training to ensure the participants are engaged. For a professional coach, we go beyond the transactional and obvious but go deep where we relate to our eyes, ears and other senses, such as kinaesthetics. For me, this is another area where coaching overlaps with both my coaching and manufacturing experience. One of the lean skills on the shop floor is deep observation, where we take everything physical we see, fully using our peripheral vision. I deliver workshops on deep observation in the context of both productivity and safety. All these are primarily for consultancy; I always find the team dialogue that happens as part of the workshop also raises the energy in the room significantly.

We have talked extensively about the importance of self-awareness and the relationship with the working culture and/or environment. Let us now turn to the physical environment. I first experienced this in facilities management back in the early 2000s and saw the influence it can have on personal productivity, particularly in open and communal space vs. closed offices. I am not going to discuss the merits of the options here, there are plenty of studies on that. However, recently I did experience what I considered to be a negative or oppressive working environment. On the surface, it was a lovely place to stay and work: a five-star hotel in a smart area in a sunny location. However, after working continuously in the hotel for a period of two weeks, while I was completing a long report, I found my energy levels diminishing over time and with it my personal productivity. This hotel was a classed as 'designer boutique'. The walls were faced in dark wood everywhere, with very low lighting levels. Not only in the restaurants, lounge and communal areas but also in the bedrooms and meeting rooms. I found I was working for progressively shorter periods and taking longer breaks. I felt I was in a negative spiral. I have noticed how this can be defeating over time. I was conscious that on long consulting engagements you can get 'cabin fever' but this was different, the physical environment clearly had an impact. When I spoke to my other associates, they felt the same, and we moved to a different hotel. The physical environment can affect personal productivity and team dynamics – something to consider on a change management programme.

There are some key requirements for clients to be coached. They must be in an appropriate mental state, with no current health issues, which could block them achieving their goals. Furthermore, we were guided very clearly, on both sets of training, not to engage with any client who may be showing the symptoms of mental health problems. These should be referred to an appropriate professional. This is another reason why a coach should be part of a professional body, as is clearly stated in the code of ethics. The next element is very critical. Coaching is not about knowledge transfer, but is a facilitation process. The client must not be perceived by the coach as an empty receptacle for the coach's knowledge and experience. However, they should be adaptive, creative, curious and ready to be coached, and in a way that they feel supported and engaged. Finally, the client needs to be prepared to shift themselves, whether it be in thinking, a belief system or by modifying their behaviour. In short, they are capable of growing and moving to a different place.

A professional coach must have some fundamental skills, particularly the ability to actively listen. Listening goes beyond hearing tacit information. A coach is required to actively listen, which means being engaged in the conversation, reading all the signs, both verbal and non-verbal. An excellent coach can also intuitively listen, which means they are able to connect all the signals they are picking up and build a powerful picture. Other experiences and skills can help this. Although I have not been formally trained in the Myers–Briggs personality test, or MBTI, having had my own assessment completed on a couple of occasions and having done some reading, I understand the concepts. It was interesting: I was discussing with a consulting associate our own MBTI profiles and the differences between being ENTP and ENTJ, which are two of the 16 different personality types in Myers–Briggs.[9] I could clearly see the 'J' (Judging) in him versus the 'P' (Perceiving) in me. Another interesting factor about the power of coaching is the fact that once your awareness is raised generally or you have an understanding of a theory or concept, your ability to see more becomes greater, and you build greater cognitive connections. I observed an associate recently, and I immediately linked it to their 'J' (judgement). I am not sure I would have made the link as quickly without my coaching skill.

Coaching structure, approach and change management models

We have seen similarities between some of the change management models. Without dissecting each model in turn, we can loosely make analogies and find commonalities between the stages of the models for the purpose of helping us determine the coaching approaches/styles at each stage. To help us comprehend better, I have grouped these common stages of the models as follows:

Stage 1 – Awareness and Recognition (needs to work differently)
Stage 2 – Getting Buy-In
Stage 3 – Determining the Team and Getting Initial Engagement (Leaders and Change Agents)
Stage 4 – Planning and Staffing
Stage 5 – Executing and Implementation
Stage 6 – Validating, Reinforcing, Sustaining

Stage 1

If we take the first stage, it is safe to assume that there has been some level of recognition at senior leadership level because there will have been a key strategic requirement or business driver. The challenge at this stage will be getting critical staff on board and raising awareness within the organisation. There will be processes that will be enacted, such as team briefings and communications. There may be existing systems, proformas, etc., available from learning and development, but key leaders may have to be guided and coached on how to use them. We cannot assume that leaders know how to do this, even if they do have the requisite skills and emotional intelligence. Setting the tone at the start will be critical, and there have been many communication mistakes or blunders, especially if the planned changes will materially affect staff of departments in terms of work type or compensation. At this stage, my coaching style would be a combination of raising self-awareness and direction. I would be facilitating sessions that enabled the clients to think about the importance of the left and right brain characteristics. I would be looking for them to raise their awareness of the perceived and real impacts of the changes to staff and the organisation, and their potential consequences. This would act as a calibration for them, and a check and balance that they had delivered the message in the right way, such that it could not be misconstrued or misinterpreted. I would probably guide them on how to deal with negative feedback or difficult questions. I once witnessed the worst delivery of a redundancy message and site closure to staff in the late 1990s. Under pressure of valid questioning from staff, the managing director tried to relate the situation to his own position and challenges as a means of raising empathy for the fact that he had to deliver the message! As you can imagine, this did not go down well. Some prior coaching in this situation would have helped. The directive element of the coaching would be to help with the preparation and planning to ensure the messages, communications and awareness campaigns and communications are well structured. Typical approaches in this phase could be visioning, planting seeds, and the use of metaphors. Best results will be delivered if the leaders and those raising awareness can deliver the key messages with passion.

Stage 2

Getting buy-in from staff will require a level of persuasion and influence. The actual coaching style will be determined by many factors, such as the company culture or the potential for resistance to change. In this scenario, we are coaching the leaders and change agents to deliver the buy-in effectively. Our style would be more persuasive, but subtly in the way that the client or recipient feels that they have some level of influence. Any type of 'show and tell' approach is more likely to generate resistance, even if it did not exist beforehand. People need to feel that they are part of the solution rather than part of the problem. It may also be important to recognise the past before we push the vision of the future. Senior employees may be vested in the past work for good reason, as they have seen the benefits for the business and themselves. They will need to understand they have to let go. Fundamentally, the buy-in process must relate to the business change, but if there is an opportunity to honestly and fairly elucidate the personal or individual benefits this will speed the buy-in process. At this stage, I would be considering coaching processes that may include visioning, seed planting, metaphors, circle of life and taking accountability. As with any coaching process, it is important that it is authentic, and the expectations are realistic. It is critical to stress the importance of staff taking accountability. I have witnessed on numerous occasions where change programmes have been initiated and the importance of taking personal accountability has not been stressed enough. There is a huge risk in these situations where staff feel alienated or disconnected form the process. They see it as a management initiative, which has been executed by others on them and their colleagues. In this scenario there will be low levels of engagement with a risk of poor execution and minimal chance of sustainable success. It is also important not to oversell the benefits of the change to the individuals as well as the organisation. I remember one situation, where a new travel expenses system was being implemented globally, and it was being digitised for reasons of productivity and cost reduction. It was sold to the staff on the basis it would make lives easier, faster approvals, less paperwork, etc. I recall a level of cynicism at the time because similar promises had been made before. The new system did not deliver benefits to the employees, as hard copy receipts still had to be retained, logged, scanned and posted, because of corporate accounting requirements. It is fine that the company had to do this, but do not raise unrealistic expectations. A coach can play a vital role in calibrating this. Coaches, like the leaders, need to be capable and credible. Capability comes from skills and experience, and credibility from previous change projects. This is where using senior coaches at this stage will be beneficial, especially if there are senior stakeholders who need convincing. Further consideration should be given to external coaches, from corporate agencies or outside the organisation.

One final reflection. At this stage, often there will nothing tangible to share with staff as the change process will be in development. This means there will be a level of faith expected from the staff. It is important that this point is made clear to them, and that more information will be shared going forward. However, do not expect staff to have faith in a process or outcome that you know you cannot deliver on. If we refer to the Kotter model, getting early buy-in and raising awareness will expand the guiding coalition.

Stage 3

One could argue that stage 3 and determining the team should come further forward in the overall process. For the exemplification of this phase, I have assumed that this is a significant change or transformation, where large teams are required to influence or execute revised processes and systems. It assumes that the initial stakeholders and influencers have been identified at the very start of the process.

This is about determining the wider execution and engagement of delivery teams. At this point the leadership will be considering the key outcome of getting rapid and effective traction during execution. Team selection will be critical; and the skillsets required will include passion, engagement, communication, presentation, planning and focus, to name a few. Depending on the sophistication and maturity of the organisation, this data may be readily available within the HR department or function. However, in my experience, even with the most sophisticated appraisal and capture system, some useful information is always missing. Talking to other potential change leaders can prove invaluable. Change agents will need to 'feel comfortable at being uncomfortable', that is, they will have to get used to constant change and supporting the ethos and methodology. They need to be curious and have a questioning mindset, without showing any antagonism or disrespecting the goal. If they see something going awry, they need to call it early. They will be team players and supportive of their teams, particularly when they are struggling with the change. Ideally, they should be well respected. If they are new to the organisation and do not have a local track record, then they must show the potential to gain credibility quickly. They will be quick decision-makers but not rash, and should clearly understand the difference between a decision and a dilemma. With these qualities they will be able to enable and accelerate change. In addition to being able to lead their teams, they need to be able to hold their own at the management table and fight their respective corners if required.

Hopefully, this has provided some insights into the calibre of the people who are required to lead and support change. Stage 3 is a vital part of the process.

Stage 4

The next stage is all about the planning of the work that needs to be done, putting the right people in the right place and delivering an execution plan. If we refer to Figure 3.2 on p. 20, this is like the execution and installation section. During installation and execution of a construction project, we need multiple large teams working to a detailed daily plan. Generally, a change of business process will not require such large teams and such a detailed plan, but the principles are the same. If this bit goes wrong, you can waste a lot of time and money. This is the point at which significant resources are committed. It is important that you have the people with the right functioning capability on each team, based on skills and experience. Furthermore, they need to have the necessary personal characteristics and communication skills, and in particular should be able to handle stress. In this case, a lead coach would be helping the leaders identify the skills criteria beyond the functioning, technical, financial or IT skills. A lead coach would probably introduce the concept of RACI (Figure 2.3 on p. 10) to aid the communication, the understanding of responsibilities and avoid confusion. Opinions are divided on the value of RACI, some see it as pointless or self-serving. In theory, these charts should be kept evergreen throughout the change or project lifecycle. This is what can lead to frustration and stress. I use RACI, but as a thought provoker and an initial alignment tool, as I find it helps get clarity, and once done it is something that can be referred to. That way, it does not become self-serving.

At this point we have put the staffing in place, and it is probably good to aim for 80:20 in the first pass. The next stage is the planning. Although the level of detail required won't be as much when rolling out a new HR system as, say, a construction project, for example, implementing a new MRP (Materials Resource Planning) or computing system that changes the way in which people work will require a level of detail. At the point of staffing, consider an independent planner who can co-ordinate all the workstreams and have an overview, and generate all the detailed plans. This should be fully integrated, and resource loaded. Microsoft Project can be used for moderate numbers of activities, up to thousands. Unfortunately, I have seen many a change process fail at this stage, because of a lack of appreciation of the necessary detail and proper oversight. People will attempt to manage in a spreadsheet or on white boards. That will work for a small number of daily activities but no more, thus there is no overall logic or integration. In one case I saw a project delayed by twice the initial planned period just due to poor planning. Once this has been prepared, the coaching style would be very much around holding teams to account for delivery, and a coach would need soft skills and some functioning skills. I have recently seen coaches brought in at the start of this phase or between phases to ask the difficult questions around accountability, and ensure the teams are functioning correctly and with the level of focus required. This quite often happens in consulting transformations.

One reflection on staffing. As the teams are formed, these truly need to function as teams. This is not to be a collection of high-functioning individuals but a cohesive team. Although the team members will have been selected for their functioning skills, they will also be expected to act as change agents. It is important that these team members and change agents can act in a 'safe zone'. In this context a safe zone means somewhere where their interactions and opinions are protected without fear of retribution, ridicule or reprisal. Delizonna, in her 2017 *Harvard Business Review* article, refers to the need for psychological safety for change agents.[10] They need to feel protected by their leaders so they can push personal boundaries and explore unconventional ideas. Personal 'comfort zones' will be pushed to drive change and learning. In his book *The Power of Habit*, Charles Duhigg refers to the work done by Google in 2015 on Project Aristotle, where it was investigating team performance.[11] Google discovered the importance of the powerful team dynamic as a measure of team performance, not just the capabilities of the leaders and the individual capabilities of the team members. It found that one of the key determinants for team success was psychological safety. This meant within the team there needed to be a level of social sensitivity built on emotional intelligence and everyone had to have an equal voice, that is, no overbearing characters. In all my consulting and coaching experience, wherever the location or circumstance, I have seen the absence of psychological safety as a major detractor from team performance, and the ability to drive change. Overtly hierarchical team dynamics regularly crush creativity and problem solving. In extreme cases I have seen them repress valid opinions on potential risk, leading to a potential failure of the change. This can also happen in very dynamic consulting environments where the correct decisions must be made quickly. The insertion of a quality coach into one of these teams will make a difference, as they will be able to recognise when the necessary psychological safety is not being observed.

Stage 5

At this point we move on from staffing and planning to execution. As we move through the journey, the activities will inevitably become more transactional. This is the point where the initial plan will have to be followed and developed in more detail. As the teams will be involved in cultural shift and business process change, the plan will be continually evolving. A coach at this stage will be helping to hold the individual team members to account for their tasks and activities. The coaching style will be more directive. The coach will be observing and listening too, to ensure that the team members do not get too tramlined either, as the plans start to evolve and there is a need to change. Easily updatable visual boards, whether electronic or physical, can help here. The critical point is that the logging and updating process takes minimal effort, so the team can focus on the change activities. When I am leading change or transformational efforts, I prefer a physical board rather than an electronic one as it promotes a level of emotional buy-in as well as cognitive processing. Obviously, this works if teams share the same space or proximity. This is not always possible with global transformation projects where electronic team rooms will be required. The younger generations are more comfortable with electronic team rooms. There is a chance with a wide age demographic that the selection of the tool might create some stress. This is another reason why having an environment of psychological safety is so critical, so that everyone has an equal voice in the selection of the tool. If you were a coach working with this team, you would have to help the process that allows the team to make the selection, but also ensure that it is clear that once the selection is made, it is followed through, even if it is not universally accepted. It is important that no team members carry what I call 'decision baggage', i.e. dwell on it afterwards if the decision did not go their way. Whether it be monitoring tools for change processes or actual day-to-day activity, I have seen plenty of systems fail, particularly electronic ones, because people can become overloaded with data or detached from the real purpose of what it is trying to achieve. In this complex digital world, electronic tools are essential for productivity but be aware of the dangers of unnecessary complexity. Physical sign-off, as opposed to electronic sign-off, of any critical or high-risk activity is generally advisable. Tools like 'Adobe DocuSign®'[12] can allow the churn of documents faster but can encourage people not to read what they are signing. I remember talking to an IT associate who is never surprised how few people read an End User Licensing Agreement (EULA) on software or app use. This is not a change process example, but a year back, a guarantor document for my son's house rental arrived electronically and asked for a signature electronically. I skim read it first and was not happy with some of what I considered to be punitive or inequitable clauses. I printed it, changed the punitive clauses, signed it and forwarded it on. I never heard of it again.

The execution phase is the one where you are most likely experiencing resistance to change, as you will be delivering change activities or helping others, which will be changing the working environments or work activities of employees. Coaches need to be aware of the potential resistance and guide the teams to be aware too. As a coach, I will always run an initial alignment session with the teams, preparing them for potential resistance and how to deal with it. I will ask them what sort of resistance to expect, as part of a structured brainstorming. At this point we would probably do a stakeholder analysis as well. It is important to know who the supporters, the neutrals and the potential detractors are. Any stakeholder analysis needs to be evergreen. I have seen many transformation projects where the change teams have lost sight of their key stakeholders and the change process struggles. I am involved with one in the Middle East at the time of writing where personnel and organisational changes have happened, meaning that key stakeholders have changed. As both a consultant and coach, I have guided the project leader to engage with the new stakeholders. This also can be a stress point, as it should mean disengaging with some of the old ones. The stakeholder cohort cannot increase ad infinitum, and it may mean some difficult conversations in a respectful tone with the outgoing ones.

Stage 6

This stage is about sustaining the gains and cementing the improvements. The sustainability phase is quite often when a change programme can fail. Too often 'victory is declared too early' and if teams have seen effective and constructive change, there is a tendency to reduce the effort and back out of this phase. Humans have a natural disposition to ease off when they feel good about something, the endorphins, sometimes known as the 'happy hormones', kick in. The initial design for the sustainability phase should be considered at project inception. It will probably be high level but there will be an outline of significant sustainability KPIs and metrics in the form of a matrix. This will not be the finished article because due to the very nature of change, work elements and activities will not be as originally envisaged. This is the point where experienced coaches, consultants and leaders familiar with change and cultural transformation will come together, process the outcomes and determine the metrics. The coaching style will be one of facilitation. Like a stakeholder analysis, this process should be evergreen, but the intensity of review and checking should increase as the change journey unfolds. The metrics will become more defined as this happens. The definition of these should be at least 70 per cent as you enter the execution phase, and as near to 100 per cent as possible as the sustainability phase starts. When setting up the metrics there are key questions to be asked:

- What will be the visible signs of material change to the outside world and those uninvolved?
- What are the visible shifts in mindsets and behaviours?
- Are staff and leaders role-modelling the new behaviours?

- Are the new systems productive and efficient? Did they meet the targets set at the outset?
- Are team dynamics productive and effective?
- Are the new ways of working inclusive and is everyone engaged?
- What are the levels of morale and have they improved?
- Are there any potential 'blockers' out there, both anticipated and undiscovered, that could inhibit sustaining the improvements?

Validation and reinforcement

The above are just a small selection of the cultural questions that can be asked to determine the correct measures. There will also be the tangible business measures too, such as customer engagement, profit, sales revenue margins, manufacturing productivity and many more. The cultural changes are not meant to be self-fulfilling but are there to support a healthy and evolving business. It is helpful to design a sustainability tracker early in the process, which incorporates the metrics you intend to use as measures of sustainability. This can range from quantifiable KPIs, such as meeting effectiveness or productivity, to more cultural ones, such as team engagement with 'smiley faces'. The ones the team uses will be driven by the business outcomes. Getting staff who have not been directly involved in the change process to be involved in the final design, presentation and visualisation promotes ownership and use of the tracker. It also gets them used to the methodology and ethos earlier in the change process. This is where coaching can play a critical role in facilitation and pose difficult questions.

It is not just about the tools. To ensure sustainable change, leaders, managers and change agents will need to validate and reinforce. Validation can take place with independent checks. I prefer to use the word assessment or validation than, say, audit, as it is less emotive. This can involve leaders visiting departments or functions, reviewing trackers, and asking open questions. Ideally, the review process should be non-confrontational, which again is where a coach can step in. It can be beneficial to bring in independent assessors who have the competencies for validation but are independent of this process.

As part of any significant change process or cultural transformation, there should be a reward and recognition process. This can be for exceptional effort or teamwork. In my experience, I find it better to avoid visible financial reward, especially as you are in the heat of the journey. Financial rewards can lead to inappropriate behaviour, upset the team dynamic or become expected. I would much rather do team events or offer trophies. However, I would consider financial reward at the end of the planned process, and only for exceptional effort. At this point, it is also important to remind teams that business transformation is an evolving process, driven by changing customer bases, markets and competition. It is important to budget for financial rewards at the start of the transformation process, to ensure that changing market conditions do not negatively influence the reward opportunity. I also used to factor this in to any construction project.

That covers the validation part of sustainability, but if things have started to deviate from the plan or intended outcomes, there may need to be a level of careful reinforcement. This can take the form of additional workshops, refreshers or motivational speeches. Ensuring that you have time, and the right competencies, to deliver this should be considered at the start of the transformation.

Coaching elements and relationships

Some further thoughts on the coaching elements and coaching relationships, both within and outside the coaching community about 'chemistry'. A positive chemistry is all about the relationship between coach and client. It goes without saying that this is one of the critical elements to success. In the same way leaders need to have patience and resolve in delivering the functional elements of programme steps, so do the allocated coaches. The more skilled the coach, the better the chance of building the initial chemistry and sustaining it. It is often reported that the initial chemistry between people is obvious to those involved and others. Furthermore, in the way that positive chemistry is immediate, negative chemistry is also obvious. It is founded on personality as well as values, beliefs and approach. These elements may have a relevance, but I would argue that a strong coach can make these elements less relevant. Strong coaches build strong relationships and chemistry by the way they behave and demonstrate their emotional intelligence. This skill comes with training, practice and experience. Therefore, organisations like the International Coaching Federation set a lot of store in these facets, with continuous professional development (CPD) programmes and experience hours. For an ACC (Associate Certified Coach), PCC (Professional Certified Coach) and MCC (Master Certified Coach), the required training hours are 250, 500 and 2,500, respectively. Like several professions, the argument rages around whether strong coaches are born or made. In the same way that I have postulated that CPD does not make a 'poor' engineer into a 'good' one, CPD and practice can make a 'good' engineer into a better one. The same analogy applies to coaching. The fundamentals must be in place before an individual starts the journey. Before I was admitted on the course for my coaching diploma, I had to have minimum academic standards but, more importantly, I had to pass an interview to assess my emotional intelligence as well as my cognitive skills and personal motivation. During my current tenure, I have been fortunate to be in the company of some excellent coaches who are in the majority, but I've also encountered a small minority of some poor ones. It is clear to see that the excellent coaches not only have the initial skills but have honed their skills over time. It is possible to be in the company of ACC, PCC and MCC qualified coaches and be able to tell the difference without being aware of their formal accreditation. The minority of 'poor' coaches usually fall into the same category, that is individuals with functioning expertise and experience in a business area but no formal coach training. Arguably, these people can add value, and are business advisors or mentors. The word coach has an extremely wide meaning and connotation, which is why the profession, which is still in its infancy, wrestles with this challenge. So why do I spend time referring to this topic? It is very simple. The main tenet of this book is about effecting change or transformation using various models and approaches while supported by coaching. It is all about practical guidance for practitioners supported by some theory. Any sustainable programme will measure itself in years rather than weeks or months and the programme will need strong coaches to go the distance.

This leads on to another point which is relevant to any discussion on coaching and the importance of having professional coaches. Coaches are trained to avoid using inflammatory or judgemental language which could be misconstrued and have a negative effect on the coaching relationship. This is also referring to the earlier point about chemistry and sustaining it. You may have noticed that I used the adjective 'strong' in relation to coach rather than another word like 'good'. This was deliberate as I believe it is less judgemental in the context of good vs. bad. One could argue that the same could apply in the context of strong vs. weak. However, in my view, there is a clear difference. In the former pair, judgement and a negative connotation could be implicit around skills rather than learning, in the latter, less so. With the latter, strong can become stronger based on training, awareness and experience. Furthermore, strong can also refer to emotional resilience as well as strength and functioning expertise. Although the differences may be subtle, they are important. A strong coach will follow those principles. This in no way implies the coach is 'soft' or politically motivated but means that they will confront issues rather than trigger conflict. This approach will support honesty, trust-building and authenticity. It will also build resilience into any coaching relationship.

I have had many experiences where this approach works. Recently in a consulting engagement, I was asked to take over a coaching relationship where trust had broken down. This is also about recognising that a coaching process is a journey like any change process, one in which trust-building in the early parts of the relationship is critical. To be clear, a coach helps their client or client team confront issues, while avoiding unnecessary conflict. This means that there will be tough talking. It is the way that a message is delivered not the message itself that matters. I have delivered the same messages as other people but in a different way, which has had a more positive outcome. It is quite interesting to be self-reflective over your previous career, and my stomach churns when I think about some of the previous dialogues and approaches I used in my younger days before my training. I am sure other coaches feel the same way when they look back on their careers. The formative years of my early career were in the 1980s when the culture was quite combative and brash, driven by money, excess and career aspiration where 'Wall Street' was regularly mentioned. I never actually sought unnecessary conflict or confronted people, but it was the language and rhetoric I used at the time. I have also mentioned previously that when we look at the concept of 'Energy Leadership', our personal average resonating level of energy or ARL is a function of our environment as well as our self-awareness. So, if I look back on those times, I can see an environmental factor, which I probably did not realise at the time. Sometimes it is helpful to reflect on the past to provide some context for the present. Fortunately, in the coaching community we see less rhetoric and inflammatory language. I have had plenty of more recent experience in more hostile and hierarchical cultures where this type of language has been used. I will discuss this in more detail in Chapter 6 on hostile cultures.

Rounding off some of the discussions on effective coaching, and the need for strong coaches and coaching practices, I would ensure there is a positive initial match between coach and client to increase the chances of success, but also recognising that coaching relationships can develop. Some client organisations like a match based on experience and status, i.e. director with director or vice president with vice president or equivalent. There are some benefits initially which can also be fruitful over time, but it depends on the skills of the coach. In my experience, clients or companies with lower cultural maturity or a tendency to be more hierarchical tend to adopt this approach. Trends are changing and some more enlightened companies are favouring a skills-based approach versus an age and experience approach. This has happened as far back as 2011, when Ernst & Young was offering what it calls a reverse mentoring programme whereby younger people with ethnic- and gender-diverse backgrounds were mentoring more senior people. It found this was a great way to open minds. This is now even more prevalent due to the fact that companies have employees with a wide span of generations, up to four and five. Similar things are happening in the coaching fraternity, with younger coaches coming into the profession. There are still age and gender diversity issues in the profession. Clearly with younger leaders, coaches are aiding them more and more.

One final reflection on change. Sometimes change happens but in such small steps we do not even recognise it. This, in certain circumstances, can be problematical. In the environs of process safety, we quite often talk about non-perceived subtle changes. There are many implementation models, as discussed in this chapter, but the success of implementation of all of them is totally dependent on the quality and dedication of the team that enacts them. From a coaching perspective, we must give due consideration to the time and intensity we spend on coaching. It is important that we do not let our passion run away with itself and deliver more coaching than we need to. I have seen this done before, and we need to get the cadence right and remember it is the client who creates 'pull'.

Reflecting on change models, coaching and true transformation

Change is not always dramatic or obvious. I regularly use the following fictitious example in workshops to elucidate subtle and non-obvious change.

> Imagine we are back in the 1980s, when times were good, particularly in the City of London, where bankers and traders were earning a lot of money. Trader James has a nice house in suburbia, the latest model 4 x 4 car, a happy home with wife and children. The market has a wobble and has lost significant money, suddenly his income is dramatically reduced. He does not think it makes sense to sell the expensive car and he loves the status it affords him in the suburbs. Servicing is very expensive, so he

decides to stop going for a branded dealer service but goes to a local garage. He needs new brake pads on the first service so arranges to have them fitted. However, the branded ones are extremely expensive, so he buys the cheaper alternative. He is faced with similar challenges on the next two services, and in each case asks for the cheaper brake discs and goes for budget tyres. One day it is raining, the tarmac is wet after a long dry spell. He is on the way back from work, going down the side streets observing the speed limit. A young girl jumps out into the road from behind a parked car. He sees the girl and brakes, but alas he hits her. He is heartbroken and reflects on his actions. Ordinarily he would have stopped in time with all the parts functioning as per design.

The moral of this story is not about car safety, but that subtle changes are not always obvious, particularly when we do not believe there has been a material change. However, over time and in combination, they can be dramatic. Being aware of and understanding the subtleties of change is critical to success. If we look at it from a positive perspective, sometimes we cannot see how far we have moved.

Key takeaways

- Any change management process, irrespective of the model that is used, must be supported by an effective coaching programme to hold leaders to account, and those who are driving the specific elements of the change process.
- As this will be a long journey, the selection of the coaches for the client leaders' and teams' chemistry is critical to success. The more experienced and appropriately trained the coach, the greater the chance of success. A strong pool of qualified coaches is critical to success.
- Strong coaches are very capable of building strong coaching relationships, supporting sustainable change. Coaching is not just for coaching's sake but is powerful with stakeholder engagement too.
- Change can happen in both very small steps and larger ones. It does not really matter whether large or small if the steps are sustainable and the approach suits the change that is required.
- There are many different coaching approaches, some of them are common to different systems; the key is that the correct approach for the individual or team is used.
- The coach needs to think about which approach is most suitable at each stage of the change management programme as well as for the individual or team.
- Coaching cadence and quality of delivery are critical, just like communication. It is possible to 'over-coach'.
- Professional coaches ideally should have similar traits to those of their key client representatives, in that they need to be curious, open-minded and prepared to grow.

- Shared experiences build bonds between individuals and team. This is critical for teams participating in a change management programme. This is another parallel between coaching experiences and participating in change. It is a reason for coaching support as part of change management.
- Be explicit in knowing the difference between 'change' and its associated outcomes with the shift in everyday activities or work practices and what is required to implement this change.
- Expect potential morale dips and resistance to change so you can plan additional coaching sessions or targeted workshops.
- Resistance to change is most likely to happen in the execution phase, so a good coach will plan for this and align the teams with brainstorming and workshops.
- Psychological safety is critical for effective team functioning, especially for those being creative around the change processes and acting as change agents. They need to be protected so they can deliver.
- Effective progress tracking is essential as part of change management or cultural transformation. Choosing the correct tools and sub-processes is also critical. Team members need to buy in to the process. A coach can facilitate the selection and buy-in process.
- Plan for sustainability of the changes at the start. Consider performance trackers and metrics. Think about reward and recognition as the team navigates the journey, and ensure you have the competencies and budget for closure, including validation and reinforcement.

6 Hostile cultures: Characteristics and potential solutions

Background

I have worked in numerous companies with a pervasive hostile environment, whether in consultancy or operational roles. The aim of this chapter is to try to help managers and practitioners recognise the signs in more depth and then prepare themselves for delivering impact in hostile environments. As mentioned earlier, there will always be resistance to change. I also believe that hostility is a relative term and exists on a sliding scale from mild to extreme. In some cases, removing hostility is the cultural challenge. I will attempt to cover some of the practical steps a leader can use to make a difference in a hostile environment, by fully understanding what is going on and maintaining focus. I will define a hostile working environment, its key characteristics, and how it can negatively impact people's abilities to work efficiently and effectively in it. It might be possible to positively influence the culture of your team, and those around you, but you may not be able to influence the company. This will be dependent on the company size and your specific role.

My reflections are from a practitioner perspective, based on experience, although I will reference some relevant research and applied theory. In addition to acting as a general guide, I would like this chapter to promote debate and challenge. Furthermore, I use the term 'delivering impact' and, in this context, it means delivering change or shifting culture.

There has been a trend in Western societies towards more progressive and less directive cultures in certain companies. In theory, employees have greater autonomy and influence over their respective scopes of work. This has been driven by a change in management practices, the belief in the value of employee engagement, and a drive to self-actualisation and the current trend of 'mindfulness'. However, I believe there have been some recent regressive factors moving away from this, in part driven by a competitive marketplace and the need to be more agile. This may seem paradoxical as conventional theory/practice has shown that a more engaged and contented workforce will perform better, and deal with the need for agility and rapid delivery. I have tried to explain the drivers for this regression. The eminent clinical psychologist Jordan Peterson, in the 2018 book *Political Correctness Gone*

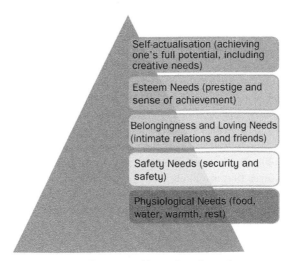

Figure 6.1   Maslow's original five-stage hierarchy of needs

Mad?, has talked about the rise of factionalism, political correctness and ultimately tribalism, and the need for people to identify with certain factions or
groups.[1] His views are considered controversial in certain quarters, as he has
approached his theories in the context of religion. In addition, he also talks about
the dangers of political correctness, in terms of its lack of transparency, and the
potential consequences of limiting open debate. To an extent this has possibly been
exemplified by the rhetoric on social media and in the press post the Brexit vote in
2016. We have also witnessed lower levels of actual teamwork in some areas and
more individualism in the workplace. This selfishness is driven by the need to survive, especially as the economy gets tighter, which is the base of Maslow's hierarchy of needs (Figure 6.1).[2]

Making a difference

The first step to delivering impact in a hostile culture is to recognise that you are in
one. That statement may sound trite, but it is not as easy as it looks. What defines a
hostile culture or environment? My definition is relatively simple. It is one in which
it is difficult to execute your work or perform consistently without thinking about
what could come next, and facing negative distractions, i.e. 'watching your back'
continually. It is noteworthy that people do not have to shout or raise their voice for
the atmosphere to be hostile.

One of the key elements for success is to understand the difference between
'active hostility' and 'constructive pressure'. The former will be intense, repetitive,
inauthentic and likely to be less rational. The latter will be effectively the opposite
of those characteristics, but will still maintain the required accountability, and

will have a level of mutual trust between parties. Typical behaviour and activities that are common in active hostility include totally unrealistic targets, minimal information, poor explanations, no context, shifting deadlines or targets and changes in scope. In more severe cases, there can be a 'mob'-style approach where a manager enlists others to aid the hostility. There are many other behaviours that one may witness, but another useful reference point is the work done by Geert Hofstede, the eminent psychologist, and his associates, on macro cultures. Hofstede categorises and describes six different cultures (see Chapter 4). There will be traits mentioned above that are pertinent in a significant number of the dimensions, but probably the most relevant are 'Power Distance' and 'Masculinity vs. Femininity'. Cultures that are likely to be hostile will have large Power Distance and show the characteristics of hierarchy, leading to existential inequality, expected subordination, autocracy, the belief that power is absolute and that its legitimacy cannot be challenged. Cultures with small Power Distance tend to be more collegiate.

One other trait of active hostility which I have witnessed is that of 'compliance'. In this case, compliance can be interpreted as compliance not with defined rules, but with dictates and edicts. Here, the end justifies the means and defined rules can be bent or ignored to meet the edict. Finally, another characteristic that will be exemplified is one of 'reactivity' vs. 'strategy'. If the rules of the game are changed, the overall strategy will become unclear or lost. Coincidentally, this also ties in with one of Hofstede's dimensions, that of short-termism vs. longer-term thinking. We must remember that none of these characteristics can be taken in isolation, and each on its own will not determine active hostility, but in combination could lead to an environment of active hostility.

What do I mean about finding the balance point, and why is it relevant? If you are a new leader in a large organisation, then to have impact, you will have to be different without either alienating yourself or acquiescing to the cultural norms too much. It is critical that you resonate with your team and conform to the rules initially. This does not stop you being a 'change agent', but you do it without being too much of an 'initial' maverick. If you are established in the organisation, this part will be easier, but for you to effect any internal change may be more difficult as there may be a reticence to challenge the status quo. The key point is that you need to be accepted by your own team to have future impact. This does not mean you do not question or challenge paradigms. It means you must effect change from the inside and gather momentum.

This is where a coaching background, or understanding the concept of mindfulness and particularly self-awareness, can help. Understanding the impact of your approach and the behaviour you arouse in the people around you will enable a greater chance of success. This will give you key insights into how your approach will impact the team as you start to challenge them. You need to find the critical 'balance point' between listening, challenging and conforming. Furthermore, you will be in a better place to understand their reactions and thus understand how to adjust your approach, if required. Finding this balance point in a hostile environment will be critical to your personal success.

Finding balance

In the previous section I mentioned the importance of finding the balance point and understanding your environs. This will be the platform for the work you are going to do and help determine the impact you will have on your team.

So, in more detail, what are the key things you need to do to have impact in a hostile environment?

- *Staying above the line* – This means as you start to challenge, never let your emotions run away with you. Stay professional, balanced and calm, even if you are getting pushback or are a recipient of some of the hostility.
- *Appropriate behaviour* – This builds off the last point, but do not let your behaviour become aggressive or inappropriate, even if some of your colleagues are being so. Do not get sucked into or acquiesce to a lower level. Inappropriate behaviour does not have to be a raised voice; it can be manipulation or passive aggression.
- *Staying true to your values* – This may sound obvious but is often difficult in a hostile environment. Staying true to your values will help your team trust you and demonstrate a level of resilience. Ideally your values should be like those of the company, but this may not always be the case. If this is true and if you wish to stay, then you may need to find values where there is common ground.
- *Be authentic* – In a hostile environment, the chances are that some of the people around you will be less authentic. Being authentic demonstrates two things. Not only will it resonate with your team and build trust, but it will show people that you dare to be different while being true to yourself and unique. Not being authentic means not being who you are because you are afraid. Authenticity is fundamental to success.
- *Focus on value, not fear* – In this context, value is not just about your or other personal values, but everything that you do is approached from the perspective of value, not fear. If we value what we are doing or are being instructed to do, we are far more likely to deliver on it, as opposed to approaching it from a position of fear. One of the examples I use regularly is that of personal protective equipment in a manufacturing environment, e.g. safety glasses. One can either 'value' one's eyes or have the 'fear' of being punished.
- *Do not be afraid to be different* – In a hostile environment it can take courage to do this, but you will reap the rewards. Some of the key and less obvious traits of 'change agents' include being on the edge continually, impatient and frustrated, and moving in an opposite direction to the herd. This requires not only inner belief, but, in a hostile environment, both patience and resolve. As a change agent you will be challenging the local paradigms, but that will not make you feel uncomfortable. The key point is to be respected, but not necessarily liked.
- *Strategy vs. transaction* – In order to have impact as a leader, you will have to be strategic. This sounds obvious and would apply to any environment.

However, you will witness an increased level of transactional behaviour in a hostile environment. In a hostile environment you will see high levels of progress chasing and transactional behaviour.

- *Confident humility* – This approach might be more difficult in a hostile environment. As a leader, you need to be both confident *and* humble. The hostility may sap your energy and the confidence that goes with it. Staff will always respect a confident leader, so this is where you will have to rely on your inner strength. The humility element will show the staff team that you are truly different, and will start to create some subliminal messages. Some people may not be able to cope with your humility and even become more hostile, but hopefully this will fade over time.

- *Helicopters and weeds* – I have used these descriptors many a time during my consultancy work to help people understand the level of detail required at any point in time to achieve the goals (see Figure 4.1 on p. 28). All great leaders can switch between these perspectives continually. Sometimes it is imperative to be looking at the detail, for instance, when you are designing or manufacturing a safety component. However, if you are looking at initial changes to a business process, then ideally you should be taking the helicopter perspective and if you were looking at the minutiae, then this could slow you down. I have seen many managers get stuck in either one view or the other, thus impacting their personal performance. So how does a hostile atmosphere negatively impact the ability to switch between the two? As mentioned previously, hostility saps our personal energy and puts us more into survival mode. The need to survive will be a distraction and can inhibit our ability to think strategically and the ability to switch.

- *'Losing it'* – Remember you are human, and although you need to maintain the utmost control of your emotions and behaviours, it is OK to 'lose it' occasionally. It shows the team that you are genuine. Behaviour is the 'tune' played by and listened to by others, because of the very dynamic and circular relationship between feelings and thoughts. Maintaining perfect outward behaviour is important, but impossible sometimes.

- *Compassion and gravitas* – It is possible to speak with both. This links to other points, but if you show compassion, you will earn respect, especially in a hostile environment. When you are demonstrating compassion, it is also possible to do it with gravitas. This will also earn you respect and show that you are serious.

- *Cognitive biases* – Daniel Kahneman has done some considerable work in this area, and these biases are real.[3] It is critical that you do not let these get the better of you, as again it increases the probability that you will make the wrong assumptions and lose clarity of purpose. A few examples of the biases that are relevant are 'Bandwagon Effect', 'Status Quo Bias', 'Anchoring Effect' and 'Negativity Bias'. The titles should be self-explanatory, but for more information and explanation, research Daniel Kahneman and his work on biases.

Relevance

Keen observers will have noted that some of the elements mentioned above are pertinent to any environment. However, the strength of character required to carry these through in a hostile environment is considerably greater. It takes character, patience and resolve to practise these and see them through. It will be impossible to practise all of these at one time, but you need to choose the critical ones for your environment. The real skill is knowing when to use them and how often. Elements like trust and authenticity must be practised all the time as they are truly transformational; the other approaches can be more in the moment and transactional. This implies another skill, which is truly understanding the difference between transactional work and transformational work. This is often confused, and people fall into the trap of believing they are transformational when they are being transactional. In a hostile environment, the probability of being transactional increases. Professional coaches and coach leaders have these attributes and skills and are more than capable of delivering effective change. It is about having a strategic plan, in conjunction with working in the moment.

I refer to Figure 4.7 on p. 49 again. The probability of one of these elements being removed is increased significantly in a more hostile environment. Therefore, as an individual change leader you need to stay true to your purpose. This is a constant challenge.

I have reflected on this earlier in this chapter, but it is *not easy* to have impact in a hostile environment so it will take significant effort, patience and a resolute approach. You will be 'rocked' by these environments.

It is important to understand that the hostile environment can grow over time, and there may be a tendency for managers or leaders to adopt a certain management style of behaviour. The environment is always fundamental as it starts shaping us from day one when we arrive on Earth, based on our personal emotional experiences and the meaning we attach to these experiences; social psychology perhaps cannot explain this in depth. Understanding the whole (body–mind) is needed; our cells have memories. If we have felt numerous times the same worry, fear etc., then every time an environment evokes these feelings, this will affect our thought processes and behaviours.

The psychologist Dr Philip Zimbardo tried to prove this hypothesis in an extreme environment with the Stanford Prison Experiment in 1971.[4] The aim was to investigate the psychological effects of perceived power, focusing on the struggle between prisoners and prison officers. He took a random group of volunteers and assigned them roles as either prisoners or guards. Early reports on experimental results claimed that students quickly embraced their assigned roles, with some @guards@ enforcing authoritarian measures and ultimately subjecting some @prisoners' to psychological torture, while many @prisoners' passively accepted psychological abuse and, following the guards' orders, actively harassed other prisoners who tried to stop it. The experiment lasted only six days, and some of the volunteers left mid-experiment. Subsequently the methodology of the experiment and its unscientific nature were questioned, especially as Dr Zimbardo was effectively involved in supervisory activities. However, from a practitioner perspective, it is easy to see how the attributes and behaviours of leaders and their teams can get exaggerated over time, with subordinates becoming quiet and submissive. I have personally witnessed both active and passive aggression[5] in these hostile environments, with the recipients physically shaking in meetings on a regular basis.

Ready reckoner for hostility

I have listed below some of the behaviours you may witness in a hostile environment as a 'ready reckoner' means of understanding the nature of the environment you are working in:

- verbal aggression
- poor adherence to standard and agreed practices
- very little communication committed to writing
- lack of clarity on objectives
- poor general communication
- constantly changing or conflicting schedules
- no praise or recognition for good work or achieving targets
- targets moving without explanation
- unrealistic work schedules
- leaders never apologising
- unnecessarily long working hours
- constant disturbance in working time
- factionalism and cliques
- passive aggression
- high value for 'compliance' at all costs
- submissive behaviour
- inconsistent HR policy or approach to discipline
- rule-based systems that are illogical, not easy to implement or open to interpretation.

One of the attributes that any leader or change agent will require is a clear understanding of their own personal self-awareness and the environment. These both impact the ability to have enough personal energy to make the required changes. As mentioned previously, professional coaches have these skills and can either coach the leaders or act as coach leaders.

In this chapter I have described some of the more extreme instances of hostility to illustrate the worst cases. Very few companies or organisations have environments like this. If you are a coaching professional and you have been engaged to make a change, then you need to be having forthright discussions with the board and the CEO before you embark on the programme.

If you are going to make change, you need to read the signs. It is critical to understand the difference between constructive pressure and active hostility.

7   Coaching challenges: What coaches will face

Context

In this chapter I will attempt to describe some of the challenges faced by coaches both personally and within organisations. At this point I will not describe the challenges in the context of the change process, but in more general terms.

As mentioned previously, coaches act as change agents and one can argue that the roles are almost interchangeable. I have compiled a list of the key characteristics of change agents and you can see how these show up in the coaching world. I will go on to discuss these in more detail as this will elucidate some of the challenges for coaching and coaches. I have pulled a number of these together from multiple sources. This will give a flavour of what it is like to be a coach or change agent. I will use the terms coaches and change agents and for the purposes of this chapter treat them the same for simplicity, even if there are differences. Coaches lead clients through processes. Change agents can do the same but can also be perceived as such by the way they handle themselves on a day-to-day basis, that is, their mindsets and behaviours.

Here are 18 typical change agent characteristics from the perspective of 'self':

1. You will always be in a process of self-development.
2. You will find yourself being alone and feeling marginal.
3. You will find yourself experiencing higher and higher levels of resistance.
4. You will get more and more in touch with what it means to 'move in' and 'move out'.
5. You will need to be caring and confrontational, guiding and directive.
6. You will keep trying to see situations with different eyes.
7. Edges of your patience will be pushed (nothing moves fast enough).
8. You will live with the tension between blending, also differentiating from them when appropriate.
9. You will be constantly revisiting your own values.
10. You will know rejection intimately.

11. You will struggle between doing what the client needs and what you need.
12. Your honesty with yourself will enable you to relate to others.
13. You will truly be yourself only when you know yourself.
14. Your greatest joy will be what you can do for others, so they can do it for themselves.
15. You will come to understand that we must care for ourselves because no one else really can.
16. You always feel uncomfortable with the status quo.
17. You see things that others do not.
18. You are not afraid to speak up when others are quiet.

Initiation

You will note that this list is very comprehensive. I will come back to it as we go through this chapter. Whenever I start a coaching engagement or assignment, I take the coaching team or leaders through a similar list. Taking them through this list helps in multiple ways. I never go through the list element by element. I always let the team read it themselves first and let them ponder for five minutes or so. I take a step back and watch their body language. I usually see some nodding of heads, raising of the eyebrows, the odd smile, and various forms of acknowledgement. This usually has multiple effects. First, it helps the team make a more emotional connection with what they are about to embark on. There is a sense of feeling rather than just cognition, validating Figure 4.5 on p. 36, which illustrates the balance between the right and left brain, or the emotional and the cognitive. When I am leading group or team coaching sessions, I guide the potential coaches to always think about the emotional side first before the cognitive, when they initiate a session. That builds trust in any relationship, which should set up the session and future sessions for success. Obviously, it is not good to dwell on this for too long. One of the acquired skills of a strong coach is knowing when and how to switch between both. A strong opening question in any coaching dialogue can be 'How are you feeling today?' It is simple but it works. It is also a good way of gauging a client's energy and/or mental state. So, getting the group to ponder on the list helps inner work, and their own emotional connections. I find that pondering on the list also helps build trust between team members through a shared experience. Depending on the size of the group, I then go through a 30- to 45-minute interactive session, asking the group members open questions, and whether any of them have experienced these feelings before. It can be an extremely powerful experience not just from a trust and team-building perspective, but also in terms of getting some insights on which change agents are likely to be 'connected' with themselves and capable of doing inner work. For extensive change management or cultural transformations, the ultimate client will want to have its staff trained as coaches. Although corporations are bringing more and more coaching in-house there is still a shortage of trained coaches. I run this session as a precursor to formal coach training. I always invite a member of the PMO (Project Management Office) or the corporate leadership team as an informal observer. It is very powerful, and for them can help confirm or question some of the pre-selections. Alternatively, it can help the PMO identify which coaches are going to be involved with which transformation teams. Finally, I always remind the leadership teams as well as the coaches that they will have to feel 'comfortable with being uncomfortable', that is, to effect change, they need to be continually pushing their personal comfort zones.

Meaning

At this point we have a better understanding of the characteristics of change agents. This will provide some context for the challenges that coaches will face on the transformation journey. These will be a mixture of personal challenges and transactional challenges triggered by the transformation journey. Some will be triggered by the coach, and some will be external factors. A coach will need to understand the differences and pick these up early. A coach with strong self-awareness will be able to do this – another reason for running the preparation session.

If we further examine a couple of characteristics from the list, this will help us understand the personal challenges. If we take number 10, which covers 'knowing rejection intimately' this relates to the fact that coaches and change agents will be pushing the boundaries constantly, but in a controlled way and hopefully without conflict. At this point it is important to stress that there is a difference between conflict and confrontation A coach will have to try to ensure that team members and teams avoid conflict, but do not shy away from confrontation. Let us go deeper into rejection; the word can mean many things, from rejection of ideas to rejection of approaches or personal rejection. For a coach, it is unlikely to be the latter, if they have the appropriate skills, however, there are times where the chemistry in a coaching relationship breaks down and a coach must be replaced or switches clients. One of the informal metrics I use for qualified coaches is how often the relationship breaks down versus the total number of relationships. A strong coach should be able to maintain all sorts of relationships in all sorts of environments. This is not an absolute indicator and there will be times where this happens in very hostile environments, where a coach will have to examine their approach. If we go back to the transformation process, this will inevitably mean new ideas and approaches. These are way more likely to be challenged or rejected by client or implementation teams. For a coach or change agent, this is where they need to have a portfolio of ideas or approaches in advance. Remember the coach is using their inner skill in coaching approaching, not pushing ideas onto the client. This is where mental preparation and planning are critical. Here I refer to Charles Duhigg's book again.[1] He refers to some work done by NASA and others on 'cognitive tunnelling'. This is where an individual can start to fixate on one or two pieces of information when overwhelmed by external triggers or volumes of information. It can be exacerbated when an individual has been in a relaxed state for a period and has lost focus. Duhigg cites an example of where a flight went down into the ocean after the pilot had suffered cognitive tunnelling. I won't discuss the circumstances, but the interesting point from a coaching perspective is what can be done to lessen this phenomenon. He discusses the power of having mental maps or frameworks with different scenarios. This not only provides alternatives or options in different scenarios, or where there is rejection, but provides a level of focus for the coach.

My approach to this challenge is what I call 'What-if' scenario planning, referencing my own mental map. I always do this before one-to-one coaching sessions subliminally or on a flipchart in a group or team context. I have two individual clients, corporate and private, where I have been through this process to help them, the latter in a relationship situation. A side benefit is that the client will also do their own mental processing. A coach will recognise rejection immediately and intimately, but with good training, experience planning and mental maps will be able to deal with it. This will also require agility as the rejections can come in quickly, particularly if the 'change team' is exploring. A final reflection on the topic of rejection. It is not just about the coach or change agent experiencing rejection, but also team members. In this case, a coach will have to guide the others on how to deal with rejection and react appropriately.

I will not cover number 5 at this point as I have already discussed the need for being confrontational in an appropriate way. I will move on to point 16, a team which deals with not being comfortable with the 'status quo'. Transformations require constant change, some in larger steps, some in smaller. A coach will also have to understand what the term 'status quo' means in the context of the programme. There will be times where a level of 'no change' is required. This could be a scope freeze within a project element. Here we mean when things start to plateau when change is hampered or stagnates. A coach will recognise this and use their skills to reinvigorate the team, help them overcome the team or individual blockers. This is where I find my training in Energy Leadership particularly powerful as this

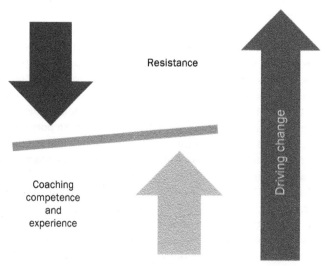

Resistance

Driving change

Coaching
competence
and
experience

Figure 7.1 The resistance seesaw

is an aid to remove blockers. This section summarises some of the challenges that the coach faces at a personal level. By reviewing the list, you as the reader will get a greater understanding of the problems. Coaches also regularly feel higher and higher levels of resistance, due to the nature of their work. This is where their training will help them to show patience and resolve.

In Chapter 6, I discussed hierarchical or hostile cultures which present their unique challenges for coaches. They will present issues on the practical challenges, assuming the coach is skilled enough to deal with their own challenges.

I would now like to talk about some of the day-to-day transactional challenges faced by coaches. These will have a more practical feel to them. These can be loosely described as various types of resistance from the client or the client's system. Figure 7.1 presents the resistance seesaw.

Three types of resistance

The resistance can fall into three categories: active, passive and systemic. All of these will cause stagnation (Figure 7.2).

The remedies required to halt the stagnation involve coaching resilience and the ability to challenge and influence.

Passive resistance

We first will look at passive resistance. This is where, for whatever reasons, the employees do not engage with the change process or programme. There can be many reasons for the lack of engagement. It can be that people do not understand the reasons for the changes properly, or they still believe they have other priorities.

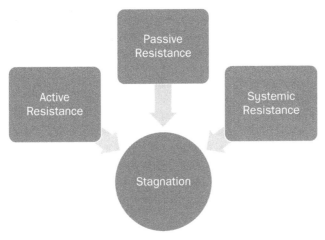

Figure 7.2 The stagnation model

If we look at the change management models, one area where we can overcome this is with the communication and awareness elements. A self-aware coach can spot the gaps early. Quite often it is not the intent that is out of balance, but the execution. The communication efforts do not deliver what they intended. The key messages could be misaligned with the outcomes. For example, if the change management programme intends to deliver new internal processes or ways of working, then the messages need to be clearly communicated to raise awareness. In short, the 'Why' needs to be properly elucidated not just the 'What' and the 'How'. Having delivered such programmes myself, and spoken to countless professionals in the arena, this is one of the key reasons why programmes fail and is clearly associated with passive resistance. If you look at PROSCI companies' own data, 60 per cent of programmes fail for these reasons.

There are other elements to passive resistance. One of the key ones is very simple and that is apathy and/or disbelief. Apathy can either be personal or collective. I have witnessed both. I will tackle collective apathy first. This can be both easy and difficult to tackle, depending on the circumstances. I tend to see more collective apathy in large companies or corporates and it is usually triggered by what I call 'initiative overload'. This is where a company is running too many programmes concurrently and the staff either become overloaded or confused or both. I have seen this many times, and I recall one global client where they were trying to run both a global behavioural safety programme, which I was involved in, and also lean programmes at various manufacturing sites. It was clear in the early interviews and focus groups, but the staff did not know which way to turn. Even worse, there was some overlap in objectives, which is not uncommon. It is resolvable if the same core teams or consultancies are working on the programmes as they can plan a level of effective integration or ensure minimal interference. If this is not the case, both programmes will probably fail. In our case, we sought clarity around scope boundaries and communications (key messages) early on. This, again, is where a coach can spot the signs, read the body language in such a way that they can ask the right questions. If staff are so apathetic, they will rarely speak up and explain there is another concurrent programme. This is clearly a leadership issue too, in terms of not understanding the impact on their staff, which comes back full circle to ensuring clear goals, objectives, scope setting and effective communications at the start. In my experience, Japanese companies are particularly good at avoiding concurrent programmes and allowing an initiative to finish or get into sustain mode before starting another.

Another reason for collective apathy is a previous history of numerous failed programmes or 'consultant overload', i.e. they have seen too many consultants in too short a period. With both cases, this is a challenge for the coach. One technique is to probe via interviews or focus groups what has failed with the previous programmes, being careful to avoid blame or castigation. The reasons are usually common and not surprising: lack of resources, lack of clear scope, time pressure, poor communication, not understanding the reality of the day-to-day challenges and many more. Therefore, an assessment phase in any intended programme is critical, as this can be fed back to client stakeholders and adjustments made accordingly. Individual apathy can sometimes be a bit trickier to deal with as it requires identification first and it is not always obvious. Individuals can hide their apathy if they do not want to be identified. This is another reason for running focus groups and one-to-ones. Running a group will surface body language. Open questions and polite probing can surface this. This is another reason why I always have an independent note taker in a focus group while I am running a session, so I can read the body language and gain engagement. Some would ask why it is important to identify individual apathy, particularly if it is only one member in a group. Individual apathy can become collective apathy quickly if the individual is an informal leader or influencer.

Active resistance

I would now like to discuss active resistance. This is where an individual, team or group is actively resisting the change. There are multiple triggers for this and, as one would imagine, active resistance is more visible. I am going to focus more on individual active resistance because, in my experience, there is less team active resistance and, if there is, it is both obvious and possibly justifiable in certain circumstances. I will discuss that later.

Individual active resistance can show up as hostility, aggression, open denial or forms of derailing. This is one of the reasons I have previously referred to the importance of doing a stakeholder analysis with the client at the start of the programme to identify such individuals. Doing a stakeholder analysis requires openness, honesty, trust and one final and forgotten element, which is sensitivity. Sensitivity is the most critical, as in any analysis you want to avoid any blame games, over-personalisation or potential character assassinations which could totally backfire. It is important to keep this process objective and focus on outcomes such as specific behaviours rather than character traits. In any engagement we usually start by looking at the organisation chart. One of the ways to depersonalise this is by using the terminology used in Figure 7.3. One could argue that the term 'hostile' in the stakeholder chart could be considered inflammatory. However, one of the critical reasons for doing a stakeholder analysis is that hostility can be a function of time and space and will be transient, depending on circumstances for the individual.

Earlier in the book I talked about the concept of Energy Leadership, where we are a function of our environment and level of self-awareness, which of course could easily trigger transient hostility. I have specifically used the word 'hostile' here to illustrate a point, in that the language we use can be very powerful in both a positive and negative way. In this case I could have use the alternative term 'open detractor'.

If we go deeper into the analysis, it important to understand the real and tangible threats to a programme, not the ones that are perceived. Therefore, in any session, it is useful to have an independent facilitator and scribe in order to maintain objectivity. As one would expect, we do not worry about the programme advocates and we would actively encourage them as change agents, just being clear that advocates can switch for numerous reasons, including lack of traction or the failure of the programme. With hostility, there are generally two approaches. First, there is coaching and, second,

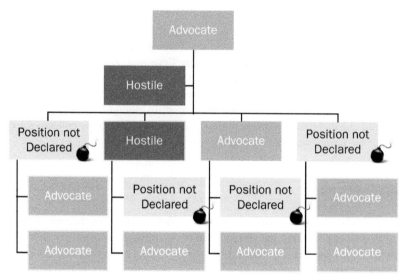

Figure 7.3 The stakeholder chart

there is isolation and, on rare occasions, do nothing. In the case of do nothing, the risks must be clearly understood. Isolation is usually the last resort, which means a move off the programme. This is to be avoided at all costs as people can change and the coaching approach is clearly preferred. There are other key considerations with detractors and that is political allegiances or strategic influence within the organisation. If we go deeper into the coaching approach, with any detractor, probing the reasons 'why' is one of the first steps. It is also important not to launch straight into coaching, as this can elicit a deeper and more entrenched position. If I am in the programme and responsible for the coaching, I will arrange for a feedback session before we get into the coaching. If the hostility is shown in the form of a negative behaviour, it is important that the person who is giving the feedback has witnessed the behaviour, otherwise it is inauthentic and will not engender trust. In the case that a senior leader must deliver the feedback, then I usually ask that they attend a meeting or session, so they can witness the behaviour first-hand. It also makes sense that a line manager delivers the feedback and not an independent coach. This is also where a coaching session will be beneficial. At the start of any engagement, I will usually do group workshop sessions for key leaders and stakeholders on coaching and feedback principles and being able to have a difficult conversation. It is possible to cover the 'why' in the feedback session, but I generally avoid it, as it can deliver a mixed message and run the risk of becoming more personal. For these reasons, I try to decouple the sessions, which is another reason for the involvement of more than one person. The most important outcome of a feedback session is that the individual's actions or behaviours are seen as unreasonable and not acceptable.

As always, the coaching approach should be open questioning, trying to understand the reasons for the actions or behaviours. It should include a clearly stated understanding of the negative impact on the programme based on the feedback session. The coach should facilitate an outcome with support that will elicit change. It is difficult to advise on how many sessions are needed, but usually two or three, if there is a clear understanding. In the case of no progress, then there is a decision on isolation. It is generally not a good idea to take an individual through this type of coaching unless there is affirmative action, and this can make the situation worse for them, reinforce a position or create unrest.

One of the most critical people in the analysis is the 'position not declared', sometimes known as the 'ticking time bomb'. In these cases, they have the potential to derail the programme, but have not declared their opinion, or it is not obvious. Here, you are trying to look for patterns of behaviours, or non-verbal clues. It is not always easy, but you can put a watch on some people if you have a hunch. Do not fall into the trap of over-analysing or interpreting, just keep a weather eye out. The process is not science.

One of the biggest failures of any stakeholder analysis is the failure to keep it current and this is usually driven by complacency. I would advocate doing one once a quarter on a multi-year programme or when you need to regroup. There are many models for doing stakeholder analysis which are more detailed and involved, where you go into the specific details of the behaviours, positions or impacts. I tend to avoid these as they can become overly complicated, overly interpreted, and run the risk of becoming self-fulfilling. This will also reduce the chances of keeping it evergreen with all the other work being done. Ultimately it is a team decision which one to use as there must be buy-in. As an aside, this leads to another point which I will discuss in a later chapter. Georgina Woudstra, the eminent team coach, talks about how high-functioning teams often determine the process to get to the outcome, not just the outcomes them-selves.[2] In my view, this is a perfect example of where the coaching or consulting team determine the model for the analysis as they will understand the context and perspec-tive. I have been lucky enough to go through Woudstra's level 1 programme.

To conclude the section on active resistance, we will cover team hostility. It is possible to do a stakeholder analysis for this, but I generally do not bother. Team hostility is usually discrete and not found in more than one team, which renders the analysis a bit superfluous. If there are multiple teams that are hostile, this usually means a systemic cultural issue, which you are already aware of and are trying to address, or there are several difficult conversations to be had with senior leaders!

In my experience, there are only a few situations where you can get actively hostile teams. To be clear, active hostility means deliberate disengagement, disrup-tion or inappropriate behaviour in a group. It is beneficial for the programme lead-ership to be clear on standards of behaviour and interaction for all teams as part of the initial communication process, particularly when there may be some harsh deci-sions regarding potential downsizing or role changes. Having a communications team mobilised throughout the programme can make the difference between suc-cess and failure. I have said team, as it is more powerful to have an expert on a team to drive standards, but also to get consensus requires more than just one expert.

In each of the cases there are some typical scenarios. First, there is the sce-nario where a team feels that they have been left out or not given attention. This again could because they are unclear as to what is expected of them and feel disenfranchised. It could also be because too much is expected from the team and they are not well resourced and choose to be hostile rather than ask for help. This can happen when they do not feel they will get listened to, or they have been ignored before. Second, a team can become hostile if they know at the end of the programme they will be materially impacted, such as loss of authority, bandwidth, freedom to operate and benefits. When a team becomes hostile, the best approach is to run a facilitated, behind-closed-doors session where the end game in the latter case is discussed openly and transparently. The session may require subsequent team coaching sessions and individual coaching sessions. In each case, it is important that the coach understands the situation but does not go into sympathy mode as that will seem trite. As coaches, we practise the concept of 'detached involvement'. This is where the coach is involved in helping but detached from the personal situation as a way of remaining objective and a strong facilitator. Detached involvement is a concept that a coach should use constantly and consistently but may need a bit more resolve in tough situations. These situations are far from easy and the coach needs to stay connected to the senior client leaders to ensure the strategic outcomes are met. The senior leaders need to ensure that they set clear expectations for the coach and are clear as to what is acceptable from an escalation perspective, as some people may have to be isolated, or change roles. In some respects, it is easier to deal with a hostile team than with a hostile individual because in certain circumstances, the work can be handed to a different team as a last resort. Whether it is a team or an individual, the coach needs to help them in the most appropriate way possible to take accountability and responsibility for their behaviours and actions.

Another key skill for a coach is risk assessment. This is not in a physical sense, but in a cognitive, behavioural and emotional sense. A coach should have the necessary skills to consider situations and assess the risk to the critical change activities, teams and individuals. This is where experience, awareness and skill come together. This is particularly important when there is a small cohort of coaches doing the work, as they will have to deal with multiple inputs and scenarios. Thinking space and the use of mental maps, as discussed earlier, will be very useful at this time.

Systemic resistance

So far in this chapter I have covered passive and active resistance. I would now like to cover systemic resistance, which is a bit different to the other two forms. What is systemic resistance? Systemic resistance is really about the in-built inertia to change, which does not relate to individuals or teams (Figure 7.4). This is where the physical and communication infrastructure can act as a barrier to improvement or change.

Figure 7.4 illustrates some of the events that can lead to systemic resistance. These are all things that should be factored in to the cultural transformation or change journey. These are real and tangible. I guide leaders on these elements at the start of any journey and if you are using a change management model such as ADKAR® or the Kotter model, these should be discussed at the first stages. The issues associated with these problems should be obvious, but I will try to briefly cover the elements.

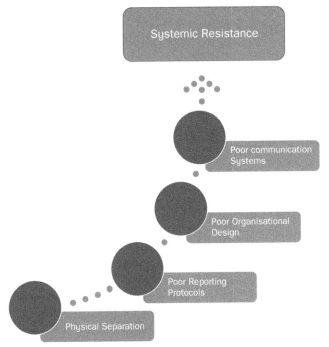

Figure 7.4 Systemic resistance model

Physical separation

The first one should be clear, and I have chosen it because in a technology-based world it is less of a problem these days. Physical separation is going to create a problem in certain cases. The word resistance may seem like a strong word, but it is just a potential blocker to performance. Resistance can become additive if the causes are not challenged and reviewed. This will depend on the nature of the business. If you are a virtual business or highly networked, then you will be used to remote working. The key point here is that if you are in a business where you need to discuss and show designs of physical things, this will be more of a challenge, even allowing for modern technology, such as virtual reality. There are no hard-and-fast rules, but I follow a simple rule of thumb, if it is at all possible I try to do all the early or strategic meetings face to face, and then work on a cadence for video and chat-rooms. From a coaching and leadership perspective, there are times when being able to view body language is critical. These elements should be up for open discussion and review with key change agents at the start. One other thing to consider is when you have a combination of both physical and virtual at the same time. For instance, there can be induced or hidden stresses for those who are dialling in individually from a remote location to those in a meeting room or board room. I know this from personal experience. There may be side discussions going on in the room that the online people are not party to. The connection may be poor. In these instances, I remind leaders to give due consideration and try to achieve a balance. This is about being authentic and building trust. As we go through the coronavirus outbreak, which is pushing more home working, these anxieties will increase. Certain business, company and regional cultures also struggle with physical separation, which again is a factor. For multi-site or global operations going through significant change, then leadership visits to sites can provide a morale boost. I do recall that during the operational excellence transformation in 2007–08, the CEO and senior leaders moved site and country locations to do their Town Hall meetings.

Poor reporting protocols

If we work our way up the tree, then the next potential resistance barrier is around poor reporting protocols. This is subtly different from communication systems or approaches. I have seen many organisations with very cumbersome or clumsy internal reporting systems. In the worst cases these have been in the form of memos or minutes. The danger is that they can be verbose, unstructured or unclear. Remember, when staff are in the middle of a change programme, the last thing they want to read is lengthy prose. On numerous consulting engagements, I have switched from complex minutes to a simple template which is focused and easily understood. I am a fan of the ABCD report for progress reporting during transformations as it is succinct and clear. It has four quadrants which cover Achievements, Benefits, Challenges and Decisions. The first two are about recognition, which is important for morale, and the last two are about hurdles, and decisions required from leaders to maintain progress. Approaches like this generate huge productivity improvements, partly because of the improved process and partly due to better energy from those involved with better engagement. These days of course there are a plethora of electronic tools available which are very effective. The most important aspect is following the principles of effective reporting. Remember, any change programme will involve multiple layers and multiple teams, which will exacerbate any reporting challenges. Keeping it simple is essential. The same applies to report-back meetings. It is about simplifying the reporting chain where possible and a lean and agile approach wins.

Poor organisational design

The third element is organisational design. This of course may be something you want to change as part of your transformation. However, I have seen many cases where this is not the core outcome, and if the organisation is not set up for effective processes, that will be another barrier. I have been involved in a recent engagement where the existing organisation was heavily bureaucratic, too many layers, thus making change very difficult. If any change is going to be effective, it is essential to have the correct organisational structure for the change which is agile and effective.

Minimise team size, where possible. If the organisation is cumbersome, this is the opportunity to role-model the new way of working in such a way that the organisation visualises the improvements and can possibly replicate them in the future. The coach's role in this is to aid the critical thinking, and support with appropriate questioning and outcome focus. The coaching team will be connected everywhere in these processes, at least initially.

Poor communication systems

The final potential resistance is poor communication systems. There is an interrelation between this and the others. I am going to give a brief mention to system, which is not the generic poor communications. The style and nature of communication should be defined at the start of the transformations and, as I have previously mentioned, this is clearly stated in all the transformation models. Here we are talking about how you reach out and communicate, particularly the systems you use, whether it is email, webinars, briefings or whatever. The leaders will know their organisation's style and culture and what is appropriate. At this point a coach can use their intuitive skills as well as their cognitive skills to set them on the right path. There is also the possibility that you can do online surveys at the start. The amount of constructive feedback that is received for improving communication systems never ceases to amaze me. This is your opportunity to get closer to the staff and build trust. There are no downsides to improving this.

To summarise this section, systemic resistance is not always considered. This is because, correctly, the leadership and coaches want to focus on key individuals and the teams as they will be the change agents. Furthermore, people want to dive into making change and solving problems without necessarily thinking about the inertia there may already be in the system. This is all about raising awareness, critical thinking and setting up for success. One final point is that the potential systemic resistance does not have to be solved from day one. Improved systems generally evolve, and this is an opportunity to follow the 80:20 rule. There are other factors that can trigger all sorts of resistance, some I have experienced and personally witnessed. I have created a simple list as reflection points. Some of these overlap with elements of a hostile culture described in Chapter 6. This is just a collection of potential resistive barriers and can be loosely categorised as psychological. They are listed under the auspices of reflection for the reader.

Elements of psychological resistance

- Fear of coaching (amateur psychologist!)
- Professional jealousy (intellectual threat)
- Loneliness and individualism
- Personal frustration
- Impatience

- Belief that coaching is just a dialogue
- Overdependence on a transactional or a consulting relationship
- Coaches seen as mentors

Key takeaways

I have generated some key learning points and reflections relating to the different challenges coaches face when they are leading and supporting a transition programme. These are designed to be practical guidance tips and easy reference points a coach or coach leader can use. They are not designed to be an exhaustive list, but to trigger thought processes.

- In any programme there will be numerous challenges for the coach, these can be split into those that are deeply personal, or triggered by self-awareness, capabilities and emotions. There are some more practical challenges that are directly linked to the change programme or transformation.
- Direct programme challenges generally come in the form of resistance which surfaces as either active resistance, passive resistance or systemic resistance, or a combination thereof.
- As a coach, you will be highly aware of your personal challenges. The skill will be in reading multiple situations concurrently in a way that you can overcome these challenges.
- If harnessed effectively, these personal challenges can spur you on to help the client more deeply.
- Stakeholder analysis is key, and it must be kept evergreen. The coaching approach and impact, both positive and negative, on any detractor must be clearly understood along with the risks.
- A vital skill for a professional coach includes being able to do risk assessments for team interactions, using cognitive and emotional processes.
- Systemic resistance to change can also be a problem for leaders and coaches. These elements are not always obvious and can cause major problems if ignored or unchecked. It is important this is considered at the start of any deployment.

8   Getting bandwidth: How to have the most impact, and be efficient with resources

In this chapter, I will go deeper into how coaches and coaching can have a deeper impact on transformation processes. If we consider again the change management models, the first stages involve raising awareness, which is the point at which coaching should be considered or even before. Coaches have a role in guiding the leadership team in key elements such as effective communications, engagement, motivation, process improvement and effective execution. In this way, coaches can support leaders setting the agenda. This is one of the early ways in which coaches can support getting bandwidth (see Figure 8.1 on p. 98). Let's look at each of the elements necessary to get bandwidth:

- building trust
- building relationships
- building networks and connecting with others
- upskilling
- maintaining energy
- building resilience
- building and maintaining credibility
- SMART and stretch goals
- taking personal risk
- daring to dream.

Building trust

One of the more specific ways in which coaches can help the leadership and project teams get bandwidth is by explaining how they can build trust and authenticity. The terms trust and authenticity are used widely these days but are critical and their use does not diminish their importance. Being authentic is clear, it is about being consistently true to your position and values, it should be immediate and evergreen. Building trust is something different, as it requires time. Trust is built over time and so is authenticity. It also requires patience. As a coach you have a dual role with

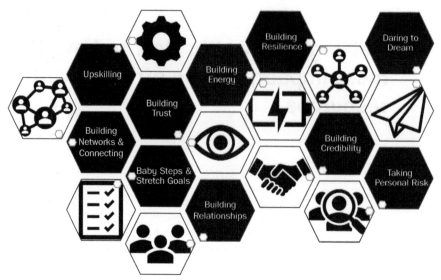

Figure 8.1 Getting bandwidth

respect to trust. First, you must get the leaders and managers to trust you. In theory, this should be easy as a professional coach who has all the necessary skills and experience. One word of caution: those who fear change may be concerned around potential ulterior motives, which will require tact and transparency, especially if you are external to the organisation. The second element is getting those who are going to be leaders or change agents to engender trust in them from their staff and teams. In my experience, one of the most critical elements is getting the team leaders to understand that it is not 'gung ho' and that they must expect resistance. How they approach their teams in a professional and considerate manner without diluting the 'change message' is what will be the critical factor. This can be addressed through a group workshop, when you can introduce concepts, such as potential resistance, morale, isolation, disaffection, and others. If leaders can talk about this openly, they have a better chance of building trust with their teams.

Some leaders and coaches deliver team-building events and workshops to build trust. These can work but the problem is deciding at which point in the programme it is best to do it. Some say right at the start, but my preference is once the team members have got to know one another a bit first as I think that builds more trust and a stronger bond. The timing will be a combination of factors, including team dynamics and company culture. The final and most important factor is to role-model the correct behaviours expected from the leaders and staff. If these have not already been defined, it is worth running a brainstorming session. It is important that these are shared with the team and they practise them consistently. It is about saying what you do and doing what you say. If you set rules of engagement, whether this be through reporting strategy or the way people interact, these must be followed through. This will engender trust even in the most challenging times. If the consistent behaviour chain is broken, trust will disappear. Some coaching schools and other bodies offer 'values' assessments. This is another way of engaging staff and building trust. Furthermore, it offers a great chance for understanding the aggregate values of your key influencers and how those relate to the values of the company.

Building relationships

Another key factor in getting bandwidth is building relationships. This may sound trite, obvious, and even like jumping on a bandwagon. We all understand that relationships are important, but building them is still difficult. Building relationships is more than just teamwork, it is about forging key links with influencers and making connections that you may need in the future. In any coaching or consulting engagement, I make a point of reaching out to those who may be beyond the initial scope or frame of reference. This is where the coaching skill comes in. It is not about pestering people but taking the opportunity when it arises. If we go back to the previous points on stakeholder analysis, it is quite easy to look at the organisation chart and work out who the future influencers are going to be, even if they are not involved in the core scope of activities. This is not about mass connections, but about engaging with the right people at the right time. That covers internal relationships on the transformation project, but what about external ones?

Building networks and connecting with others

The next element is a follow-on from relationships. Building external relationships or a network is also powerful. Many times, I have called on my external network to help both from a coaching and consulting perspective. I am fortunate to be part of many networks with access to 10,000+ qualified coaches and thousands of consultants. I have called on these numerous times, especially where they have a specific skill or experience. When this happens, it is another opportunity to forge stronger and new relationships. Collaboration is the key, and there will be symbiosis. I advocate becoming a member of the appropriate professional body and professional LinkedIn groups.

I have refrained at this point from talking about building effective teams or teamwork, because there are considerable materials available that deal with building teams, and it is a topic on its own. However, I would comment that teamwork is also critical to success and teamwork often is not as well established as we think. In his book *The Five Dysfunctions of a Team*,[1] Patrick Lencioni chronicles the fictional arrival of a new CEO, Kathryn, at DecisionTech and her journey of analysing the exec team, challenging it, then building it. In the fable, he alludes to his experience with working with CEOs and exec teams and the actual lack of teamwork. In addition to discussing the five dysfunctions model, he refers to the key point of the importance of having strong team players rather than a group of exceptional individuals trying to or pretending to function as a team. Exceptional individuals tend to be driven by ego, recognition and fear, rather than team results. I have experienced this myself numerous times in consulting and in operations. In operations, I experienced it first as engineering manager for BASF in Wolverhampton, where I had to pick up the team after a lot of previous hostility and we bonded with a common objective for effective maintenance, reduced breakdowns and increased productivity. We had to deal with some home truths, dump our egos and accept others as leader even when they were in development. While consulting in Russia and leading the field implementation in Voronezh, I deliberately spent time building the team, getting unity and common goals rather than looking at individual functional excellence. Furthermore, during the diagnostic phase, we exceeded our opportunity target ahead of time. There are other examples, and even as a functional expert within a team, I have seen excellent team leaders and poor ones. There are several characteristics that define excellent leaders, which align with the model:

- They all allow appropriate and constructive conflict.
- They get the team members to trust one another implicitly.
- They support by sharing personal vulnerabilities appropriately.
- They promote individual and collective accountability.
- They measure and focus on collective results.

Upskilling

You will start to see a natural follow-on from the above. Another critical element is upskilling and staying fresh. The professional bodies, such as ICF, AoEC and others, hold regular webinars, both paid and unpaid. For the ICF, continuing professional development (CPD) is mandatory to maintain certification. It is important to see CPD as an opportunity, not just as a necessity. From my own perspective, I look for webinars and training based on knowledge gaps. The profession is still in its relative infancy, which gives an opportunity for development. By their nature, coaches and consultants are curious and keen to self-develop. One way to get greater bandwidth is to encourage others to be curious too. I regularly post articles and share links to articles, and tag the team on platforms such as LinkedIn. The great news about curiosity is that it becomes infectious. I have mentioned before that through the process of a transformation, the coaches and leadership team have identified high potentials and future leaders. They all have curiosity and self-development in common.

Maintaining energy

Another element for effective coaching is maintaining the right energy. Again, this may sound obvious, but there is a link between our personal energy, consciousness, mental programming and our performance and personal sustainability. This is not just about physical performance. Sportsmen and women need to be both mentally and physically fit to perform. As mentioned previously, my business coaching evolved from some work done in the sports area. I am not going to cover physical fitness here, but there is a myriad of information and scholarly articles on how physical fitness can improve mental fitness. There is also a link between personal energy and resilience, which I will cover later. Our personal energy is linked to two key factors: the environment we are working or living in and our self-awareness, both of which we can influence and control. Self-awareness can be practised and will develop over time. This is all about the impact you have on yourself and the others around you. The greater the understanding you have, the greater your personal energy and the greater the impact. Your energy is directly about your behaviour or relative extraversion, but also how you see yourself in your world and that of others. If we look historically at the great leaders such as Gandhi, we note they had considerable self-awareness and presence. With this came abundant energy which allowed them to deal with complex and difficult challenges. Coaches need to demonstrate confident humility without ego. This is what we have been taught in our professional coach training, but we need to live and breathe it consistently. The more often we do it, the better we become, the more energetic and impactful we become. The process becomes additive, leading us to a state of 'unconscious competence',[2] i.e. we can guide, facilitate and lead without thinking. This is totally congruent with the intuition required by a coach.

Unconscious competence is the fourth stage of competency after unconscious incompetence, conscious incompetence and conscious competence. The first stages can be categorised as 'I don't know what I don't know', 'I do know what I don't know', 'I do know what I know' and 'I don't know what I do know'. The fourth stage can sometimes be gauged as 'muscle memory' or 'intuition'. There is also a link between the final stage and interdependence. Interdependence is where we start thinking ahead intuitively and look out for one another. This is where several concepts come together. Put simply, this is where we just experience a sense of 'being'. Bruce Schneider describes this as part of level seven energy in his Energetic Self-Perception model, where we have a core thought of non-judgement, a core emotion of absolute passion, and action or result which is creation.[3] This is what all coaches should aspire to and will help them perform at the highest level. When I am coaching future teams and leaders, I share these concepts, because I think it helps them as it connects thinking and acts as an enabler and an accelerator. This provides them with both a goal and framework for them to work with as a means of improving their impact.

Building resilience

There is a natural follow-on to the next element, which is building resilience. Having higher energy will enable us as teams and individuals to have greater resilience. These are not the only factors that help to build resilience. In his *Harvard Business Review* article, '5 ways to build resilience at work', Rich Fernandez talks about the fact that resilience is multi-faceted.[4] He states that the most resilient individuals have learned to fail rather than not failing, but fail quickly and regroup. Other business gurus like Richard Branson have recalled their own stories in this light. This is what is sometimes called 'fast failing'. In the coaching community, it is encouraged to experiment with this. In consulting, we regularly test hypotheses within a framework as we cannot predict the outcomes. This is akin to fast failing but without necessarily a major risk. Throughout my consulting and coaching career every experienced coach and consultant has had some sort of failure that has shaped them and helped build personal resilience. Those failures help us to consider risk in a clearer perspective and approach the next challenge with a reinforced framework. Fernandez also then discussed the importance of having the correct attitudes and behaviours as a means of collective and individual resilience. In my consulting experience with DuPont, we always covered this as a key anchor of any cultural transformation, whether it was a process safety or operational excellence transformation. He also goes on to talk about what he describes as 'good stress', which is sometimes known as 'eudemonic stress'. This can have a positive effect on our well-being and productivity. I call this constructive tension, and it can also happen between individuals. This also builds resilience in a way that boosts our energy on the back of well-being and productivity.

I like to build analogous links between physical science and psychology. If we take the mathematical definition of stress or tension, it is that of force divided by area. The larger the area, the lower the stress. We can liken the area to an increasing resilience. Resilience is also like a self-developing immune system for those who are fit and healthy. The problem is how people stay mentally fit and healthy. I have covered this topic previously, but the stress of hyper-connectivity and working 24/7 across the globe has been a growing phenomenon and will negatively affect our health and well-being. Unfortunately, I have seen this in the corporate consulting industry numerous times. I had to force myself to take breaks to regain a sense of control and avoid burnout, which is another factor.

Fernandez goes on to talk about the five specific measures he and his colleagues have identified that can build resilience. The first measure is the exercising of mindfulness. I am not going to cover this here, because I have already touched on it earlier in the book. The second measure is compartmentalising the cognitive load. This means we segment the voluminous amounts of data we receive so that we can process these effectively. I recall the comedian and intellectual Stephen Fry being interviewed about his expansive knowledge on a range of topics and his ability to answer questions and quizzes; interviewers were bemused by his stellar performance. His reply was clear, it was the ability to compartmentalise stored information, and easily reference it by generating mental tags for rapid recall that made it easier. Top card players and gamblers follow a similar approach. As coaches and leaders, we need to be able to do the same to some extent. If we look at the complexity of cultural transformation or change management programmes, managers faced with voluminous information and changing situations must do the same. This builds resilience while driving performance. Compartmentalising information will also aid effective delegation.

The third and fourth measures are taking detachment breaks and developing mental agility. The former is concerned with maintaining performance by observing ultradian cycles as opposed to our circadian (daily) rhythms. Again, top sportsmen and performers learn to practise this. They are careful with their training regimes in terms of timing so as not to get overly tired, and eat the right food at the right time for maximum performance. In 2015, I was lucky to meet Dr John Briffa. His book, *A Great Day at the Office*, talks about the requirement for water and proper nutrition, but also reveals the best parts of the day for working.[5] I saw him speak at an HR convention and he debunked some of the myths around wrong food types, working and the fallacy of 'presenteeism'. This is why we need to do critical work when we feel at our best. Doing this helps our resilience as it gives us a sense of achievement and a level of confidence that we are doing well. This means we can also draw on this when things get tougher.

The next measure is mental agility. This resilience skill is sometimes known as 'response flexibility'. The eminent psychologist Linda Graham[6] describes this as 'the ability to pause, step back, reflect, shift perspectives, create options and choose wisely'. This is absolutely what is required but can be developed with some training and experience. There are plenty of mindfulness-based resilience trainings available and these are highly appropriate for coaches. I know with my consulting in Russia, we actively taught ourselves to pause and reset using role play and feedback. I have talked about the concept of detached involvement before, so being present but detached helps us be more focused and impactful. It is about the mental equivalent of muscle memory, knowing intuitively how to deal with a difficult situation. The more you do it, the better you get at it. Being self-aware allows us to anchor ourselves before we work on difficult things, with a greater probability of having the 'response flexibility' which Linda Graham describes.

The final element for building resilience described in the article is 'cultivating compassion'. This is about self-compassion and compassion for others. Fernandez references research from the Greater Good Science Center at UC Berkeley which found that compassion increases positive emotions, collaboration and better working relationships.[7] I have seen this in my own work life. Even though corporate consultancy can be quite competitive, I have been involved with plenty of foreign projects where there is a team spirit as we are away from home and families. There is an extra spirit, and everyone will go through a difficult time at some point, and showing compassion for those going through those difficult times supports the team. I have also previously mentioned the importance of having a value-based culture versus a fear-based culture. One of the key outcomes for any coach, particularly during times of change, is to develop and support a value-based culture. A value-based culture will nurture levels of compassion and the process becomes symbiotic. This is what I initiated when doing some leadership work for a large manufacturer a few years back. There was considerable despondency among the team, based on some critical events. Before I started to guide and lead the team on their functional work, I started doing weekly coaching with the team, something never done previously at the site. Over time I could see the teams' interrelations start to improve. This in turn started to generate levels of care and compassion within the group, with levels of interdependency rather than individualism. With that came levels of compassion towards the others, and improved team spirit. This also aided the problem-solving capabilities and solution focus at a challenging time when production was key. Another factor in building resilience. Kira M. Newman from the Greater Good Science Center talks about the importance of self-compassion and looking after ourselves, where we confront our suffering with warmth and kindness as a means of removing unnecessary stress. Building resilience requires a multi-faceted approach. It is OK to experiment and fail as a means of building experience.

Building and maintaining credibility

The next element in having impact is building credibility. I will not analyse it in detail but merely reference its importance. This of course applies to leaders and project managers as well as coaches. There are various elements to building credibility, such as delivering quality workshops, forming lasting relationships, being trustworthy, being authentic, being helpful, being humble, being consistent, being confident and many more. These are all characteristics that will help build credibility. Building credibility takes time but can quickly and easily be destroyed. The key factors in destroying any credibility are a loss of trust, authenticity and consistency. The first two are obvious, but the third less so. I have already discussed authenticity and trust at length so will leave it there. Being consistent in any delivery or change project is critical because teams and individuals pick up on that quickly. So what does consistency mean in this context? Consistency here is about a common approach, common rules and a framework that teams adhere too. As a coach or leader, you must set the framework and be open. This is something I do at the start of any delivery. I make clear the importance of consistency and role modelling and that if they see me being inconsistent, they must feed back. This will build trust and increase levels of engagement. This is yet another example of symbiosis.

SMART and stretch goals

The next element in increasing impact is having SMARTER goals. Readers will have heard the term SMART objectives which stands for *S*pecific, *M*easurable, *A*chievable, *R*ealistic and *T*imely. This is well documented in management handbooks and company literature. What does this mean in the context of change management and coaching? In my experience this means not losing sight of the end game and following the principles of 'baby steps'. It is critical that we do not get too far ahead of ourselves and that we have a clear plan. The work that will be done by the implementation teams will be challenging. At a practical level, this means that certain elements will take longer than expected, so factor this into the initial planning without sandbagging. Ensure all the steps are logical and that the dependencies are clear. Avoid too much parallel activity even if there are tight deadlines, as critical dependencies may be overlooked. Take time to think about the emotional as well as the cognitive levels. If training is required on a topic such as 'difficult conversations', this could be quite a cultural shock to the system for some organisations. A training package should include the opportunity to practise with role play before the real activity. This is a common approach for those involved in crisis communications, which is pertinent at the time of writing with COVID-19. With crisis communications, they even run simulations and scenarios. This is very common with large chemical complexes where the consequences of a plant meltdown could be significant. I recently led a workshop session in Qatar where we did powerful role play on workplace interactions. The role play is effectively a baby step or enabler to get proper engagement. Break the workshop into effective 'chunks'. Ensure the workshop is an effective chunk for the overall programme or workstream. There is the famous cliché, 'You have to break down an elephant into steaks in order to eat it.' Effectively this meets the SMART criteria, i.e. it is important not to forget the less obvious stuff. This is another element to help coaches and teams have impact.

Taking personal risk

I would just like to take the opportunity here to talk about personal risk. Some people quite often misunderstand the term personal risk and confuse it with physical risk. In the context of coaching and management, it means being prepared to be different and accept the consequences. I have seen 'risk' defined as the potential for the uncontrolled loss of something with intrinsic value, which could be physical heath, well-being, resources or other. My definition of personal risk is 'When you are prepared to stand up for something you believe in, which is different from the current norm, accepted practice, knowing that there may be consequences that could lead to a loss of credibility, reputation or increased pressure.' Generally, this happens when you see an opportunity for an improved outcome or when you can see something going awry when others cannot.

The best way to illustrate this is by using personal examples. I was involved in a consulting and coaching delivery for a large foreign multinational. My scope of work included coaching leaders and functional staff, and delivering a series of specific workshops over a period of five or six months after completing a diagnostic assessment of the culture with the associated mindsets and behaviours. This had been defined in the overall programme. Within reason it was otherwise down to me to deliver quality work and help the overall project effort. So, thinking about the other practices and approaches I have mentioned in this chapter, I started to build my plan. I set about the diagnostic and fed back the results, which were well received. However, with a clearer picture on the culture, I decided to defer the standard training workshops. I delivered a series of workshops to engineers and supervisors on 'linewalks' or interaction-based field assessments. The key driver was to get the supervision staff into the field and out of their offices. In conjunction, I also redesigned the coaching cadence, so we could do it in the field and base it on the linewalks. The focus groups within the cultural diagnostic had shown that supervision was not present enough in the field. This whole effort took considerable time and energy, but I stuck to it, knowing that this would be beneficial in the long term. During this period, I was constantly being chased and was under extreme pressure from the leadership to deliver the other class-based modules, which I kept deferring, knowing that the fieldwork would add more value in the longer term. It worked and the levels of engagement were excellent. So much so, that the remaining modules were delivered quickly and accepted more easily. This is just a small example of taking personal risk, by doing what you believe in for the better outcome. To take this risk means that you must have levels of trust with your clients and teams. The trust element also ties in with one of the five dysfunctions of a team as described in Patrick Lencioni's book.[8] We can also see that taking personal risk is an 'enabler' for other difficult work to take place as it pushes boundaries and opens people up for more. Taking the appropriate level of personal risk will have more impact in the long run.

Dare to dream

The final section of this chapter relates to 'dreaming'. I have been trying to find an accurate and meaningful definition of the word 'dream'. According to the *Oxford English Dictionary*, a dream is 'a series of events or pictures in your mind while asleep'. In the context of coaching, dreaming means using imagination and forward thinking. It is important that leaders and coaches can dream in order to push boundaries and set the context for improvement. The key point being that this will help set stretch objectives that aid transformation rather than being overly transactional. The role of the coach here is to aid the process and help set the agenda for enhanced performance through imagination. Some coaches have a very specific talent for this type of facilitation, and it is best to use them. This can form part of a workshop or group coaching session and is usually done with senior leadership or a team with specific responsibilities for really stretching the current environment. The process of stretching can also deliver stronger year-on-year financial benefits post transformation, better than originally forecast. We saw this during the DuPont Operational Excellence transformation from 2008–12. It does require a robust measuring system and tracker. The Japanese ethos of 'Kaizen' or continuous improvement helped significantly. This is another way in which a coach or coaching can increase impact.

Reviewing the bandwidth

As we near the end of this chapter, I just wanted to briefly mention resourcing and team sizing. Team sizing will vary from client to client. If you are leading a programme, there is no hard-and-fast rule and it may depend on the number of professional coaches at your disposal. It will also depend on the balance between team and individual coaching that is required. I will talk about team coaching in Chapter 9, but the proportion of team coaching will depend on a number of factors, including the topics you will be delivering, the size and structure of the organisation and what the intended programme outcomes are. This should all be factored into the initial project plan. There may also be the opportunity to train some additional coaches to increase bandwidth, while retaining the professionally trained and experienced coaches for either the senior leadership or leaders who are taking the most challenging workstreams or activities. At the start of any significant engagement I often do a group session on basic coaching, so those who engage with others understand the basic principles of authenticity, role-modelling and building trust. In terms of coaching ratios, I generally guide on the 1:6 span of control heuristic used for leading teams. I would not go above this for a couple of reasons. First, there will be the requirement to maintain trust and confidentiality, and if this ratio is exceeded, there may be a perception, even if the correct agreements and processes are in place, that there may be leakage of information. Second, the coach must think about their bandwidth and the ability to coach numerous individuals effectively. Typically, I try to aim for a maximum of four if possible. The other factor is how many sessions to run per day. The majority of coaches book one-hour slots for personal one-to-one sessions allowing for, say, 40–50 minutes with a gap at the end for close-out and recap. For large transformations I would not expect any more than three sessions per day (four maximum) as a means of maintaining focus and energy. It is important to have gaps in between the sessions to reflect and regroup. It also allows for overrun for important sessions. As an aside, within the personal coaching arena I never ask clients to pre-book too many sessions in advance or run a system of packages. My coaching approach is to have a minimum number of sessions in order to get initial traction, create value in the moment and then reflect after each session. We proceed on the basis that the client is getting value until a natural end point.

A final note: coaches should plan well in advance of any delivery on how to deliver the most impact and sustain the changes. This will involve an appropriate combination of the practices and approaches mentioned in this chapter. Adopting clear rituals for consistency will have a real benefit. As always, there is no single element that will deliver the increased benefit, but an appropriate combination. This combination will evolve over time and it will be the skill of the coaches to identify what is relevant and when.

Key takeaways

- A coach should work out the best means of having impact at the start of any engagement and co-develop the plan with leadership. The coach can ask the challenging questions and help them with imagination.
- Building team and individual resilience is critical. It is multi-faceted and involves personal and inner work. It is OK to experiment as a means of getting experience.
- There are means of building and maintaining energy to have greater impact; practise what works best for you and let your team do the same.
- Taking personal risk takes courage and needs trust, but will increase the levels of overall impact.
- All the individual elements required to build resilience are symbiotic and support one another. We can liken these to the structure in Figure 8.1, which shows them forming a strong honeycomb.
- The process of 'stretching' needs to happen throughout the lifecycle of the transformation, with regular check-ins on performance and re-imagining where necessary.

9 Team coaching vs. individual coaching

Opening

So far, I have not really discussed the benefits and pitfalls of team or group coaching versus individual coaching. Both have a place in any change management engagement. A further reflection is that this book is not intended to be a coaching manual or a 'how to coach' book but is more a text on what are the key outcomes of coaching, and how can it be effectively integrated into any change management or cultural transformation programme? Before I launch into more depth, there are nuances and obvious overlaps between individual and team coaching. There are many different definitions of team coaching, but the fact that there are so many different definitions proves that the area is still relatively new even though there are numerous books and texts on the subject. Coaches are still finding their feet, developing models, sharing knowledge and developing their skills. This was discussed at length during the 2020 ICF Conference and particularly that team coaching is still in development.

Both team and individual coaching can be very specific. As I have mentioned before, in the case of individual coaching, the agenda should be set by the client. In the case of a transformation project, this should be within the context of the overall transformation outcome. For example, if the transformation is for improved sales and marketing performance, potentially using more digital systems versus more personal face-to-face engagement, by helping to overcome the fear of using computers. In the context of operations, it could be the fear of having to do presentations. These are just two examples, but I have witnessed both. Sometimes you will understandably get personal requests that are not related to the goal but are a real challenge for the individual. At this point, we should try to avoid judging or saying that the topic is not relevant. Quite often, these topics do have links to the core outcome and these are worth exploring. These generally are the areas that are required by individual coaching.

With any form of coaching, whether it be individual, group or team, building trust or using the terminology 'co-creating the space' is critical. Any coach leading or being involved in a transformation programme should read or refresh their memory of the ICF core competencies, which are available https://www.coachingfederation.org.uk/credentialing/icf-core-competencies. This is a good reference point for centring and anchoring and is available for non-members.

Before we go into the pros and cons of team coaching versus individual coaching, a brief note about group coaching. Often team and group coaching are confused because of the similarity of the terminology. I do not intend to cover anything in depth on group coaching because there are not so many opportunities for group coaching in cultural transformation. That does not mean that these opportunities should be precluded.

Group coaching

Group coaching is about getting the team to work together as they have a common interest in solving their own specific challenges. This is done by listening to one another, and building on and challenging one another. The role of the coach is to hold the space in a way that allows team members to do that. Outside the context of change management or large-scale cultural transformation, this is an efficient way of coaching those with a common interest. Another way to look at this is just coaching individuals within a group. As an example, a group of managers within an organisation may have a common interest in engaging with their teams, but will find different ways of doing it, which could depend on the nature of what each department does. It is not an area I have invested in so far for the reasons mentioned above. Furthermore, having spoken to other corporate coaches, it is not an approach that is widely used. To give an indication of how this process works, I have shown an illustration of the model in Figure 9.1. As with the other coaching approaches, it is the responsibility of the coach to hold the space for the others to listen, work, challenge and debate. I will mention it again later in this chapter but Alexander Caillet discusses two different group modes and three different team modes in his article, 'The team adaptability advantage'.[1] The two group modes are leader-directed and working group, with the three team modes being leader/member, rotating /shared and self-directed. This is a useful link between team and group coaching or working. Another explanation for group coaching comes from Georgina Woudstra in her article 'Coaching individuals in a group context such as in action learning sets'.[2] This provides a different perspective which helps

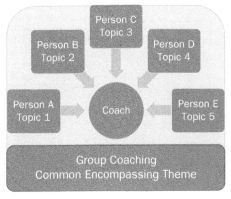

Figure 9.1   Group coaching model

understanding. Even established professional coaches are coming to grips with the differences between team and group coaching and must constantly remind themselves to be effective while working in either context.

Individual coaching

I am not going to spend too much time talking about individual coaching in this chapter, because I have previously referenced numerous coaching approaches for one-to-one engagements. Furthermore, as I have also mentioned before, it is not the intention of this book to be a manual of coaching. However, I would like to mention one model that simply summarises key elements of the individual coaching process from end to end. The reason for doing this is to give the reader an idea of what is entailed, but I am not advocating this over any other process.

The GROW model[3] highlights a four-step coaching process (Figure 9.2). GROW is an acronym for *G*oal, *R*eality, *O*ptions and *W*rap-up. This is an adaption of the original model which has the final step as Wrap-up as opposed to Will, which I prefer for reasons mentioned later. I also like this because it is a great way of showing the client how a coaching process will work. There are still some people who fear the coaching process as they see it as potentially judgemental or as psychoanalytical in some way. Even though coaching can be an intuitive process, being able to show the coaching journey in a more transactional way helps some. I have highlighted throughout this book my passion for productivity and 'lean' thinking. One of the recognised lean and quality approaches is PDCA, or Plan, Do, Check, Act, which is a very powerful approach for being focused and staying true on small bits of work or micro projects. PDCA never stops, because once a cycle is complete, then it is a series of repeats. Hopefully, you will see the analogy not just in the similar stages and structure between PDCA and GROW, but also in that coaching never stops and must be repeated. Another reflection on the GROW model is that the process gets both coaches and clients to engage with the processing and logic sectors of the brain as well as the emotional and intuitive sides of the brain.

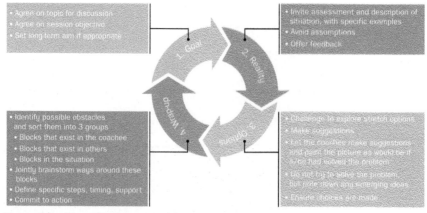

Figure 9.2 The GROW model

A final thought on the GROW model in the context of individual coaching: it can also be used as an overarching model for 'teams' in the context of large multi-faceted engagements. If we look at the transformation journey, the project must have a *goal*, it will need to be cognisant of the *reality*, explore *options* and then *wrap up*. This thinking is in line with any of the change management models such as Kotter's 8-step, ADKAR®, etc. mentioned in Chapter 5. Furthermore, if we can implant the GROW mindset and process within our delivery teams at the start of the journey, we have a greater chance of success. We need to plant the seed continuously, actively and subliminally. Let us consider this as part of the 'repeat cycle'. This hopefully is a segway to my section on team coaching.

Team coaching as support for cultural transformations

Background and preparation

Team coaching is different in that it involves coaching individuals who are all working to a common goal and usually with a common approach. This is highly relevant and suited to large change management or cultural transformation programmes. In their book *The Wisdom of Teams*, Katzenbach and Smith define a team as 'a small group of people with complementary skills who are committed to a common purpose, performance goals and approach for which they are mutually accountable'.[4] There are many other definitions, but this resonates with me as one of the clearest and most easily understood. It is also important to understand that team coaching is not the same as team facilitation. These are often confused, particularly as team coaching is still in its emergent phase. Coaching is all about co-creating the space for the team to grow and flourish in their own way, guided by the team coach with appropriate interventions. Facilitation has a lot more emphasis on the process within the team or group. Effective team coaching also requires multiple phases of 'contracting', that is getting pre-agreements with both the client sponsor and the team at the genesis of the coaching process.

I regularly use team coaching as part of change management programmes or cultural transformations. Typical transformation programmes in manufacturing can be operational excellence, capital excellence, process safety and behavioural safety. Team coaching can be used either as standalone topics or as a means of supporting workshops. Figure 9.3 shows the relations in team coaching.

Numerous books and papers have been written on team coaching. They all have some common principles, which are useful to explore without going through an anthology of team coaching. I have tried to distil some of the principles into a consolidated list. Before I do that, it will be worth thinking about what makes an effective team. If we refer back to Figure 3.5 on p. 25, it shows the sort of skills and experience blend that is required for a high-functioning team. The typical characteristics of a team are:

- it has clear direction
- it is focused

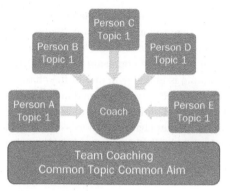

Figure 9.3   Team coaching model

- it is balanced in terms of skills
- it is balanced in terms of diversity
- it is structured with a clear agenda
- it is adequately resourced
- it understands its objectives and its agenda.

The above list shows the fundamental aspects of a constructive and effective team. Often, there is a tendency to launch into team coaching without getting the fundamentals in place. When planning to coach a team, I will always ask questions to ascertain the above. This is not the time to get over-analytical but to think of the 80:20 rule. When doing the prep work, I usually investigate elements that easily get overlooked. Furthermore, it is likely that you will cover some of the elements such as direction, structure, focus and objectives as a natural part of the coaching process. Hopefully, the team selection process will have ensured a suitable balance of tangible skills. The two biggest gaps I see are (1) resourcing and (2) diversity. In Chapter 2, I talked about the RACI diagram (Figure 2.3). This could be a good time to introduce the concept and discuss it.

Teams and their leaders tend to assume that all the resources are in place before they start and often this is not the case. What do we mean by resources? Resources means not only access to materials, communication systems or support personnel, but also their own mental support resources. Support resources can often be the biggest challenge as these days they are often shared. We are long past the days of the typing pool, and with the advent of PCs and planning tools we are generally expected to do things ourselves. Away from typing, there are numerical skills, spreadsheeting and even making presentations visually appealing and engaging. There are many others, but I always generate a checklist with the programme leader or delegate it to one of the team. If team members are going to develop their own materials in all areas, then a training plan should be developed to upskill on project management tools like MS Planner. Other considerations include whether everyone is on the same IT platform or using standardised tools, however this should all be sorted at programme start. This all sounds obvious, but I have seen gaps and the

COVID-19 crisis at the time of writing has highlighted differences in video communication channels within organisations and their sub-divisions, such as Cisco vs. Zoom and MS Teams. I will not expand on my previous comments on the need for psychological safety, just say that teams need it, and consideration must be given to the magnitude of resources. One of the reasons that support resource is quite often overlooked is that the remit of teams has a natural tendency to expand as work develops.

When I talk about diversity, I mean diversity of thought here in addition to gender, culture or background. I highlight this because it is less visible than the other aspects of diversity. These all are important, but it is the neurodiversity mentioned in Chapter 3 that is critical. Team members who think along the same lines are more likely to have a sub-optimal result. In her interview with Evan Apfelbaum, published in 'The trouble with homogeneous teams',[5] Martha E. Mangelsdorf describes several of the performance downsides of homogeneous teams, including cooperative decision-making with less creative solutions. Furthermore, Evan's research yielded that homogeneous groups were less likely to make wise purchasing decisions. At the time, his work related more to race, gender and culture, but the general point about homogeneity holds good. As highlighted in Figure 3.5 on p. 25, diversity drives a necessary creative tension in a team. I always worry when a team comes to a consensus too quickly. Practically, how can we ensure a level of neurodiversity? There are of course no assurances, but a simple informal interview of the team members can help, where you ask a few questions. Typically, these questions can be:

- What do you find most disruptive in a team?
- What are the most irritating habits of team members?
- When you are on your own, how do you arrive at a difficult decision?
- Describe some of the cognitive biases you have witnessed before.
- Do you consider yourself more emotional or analytical? Describe why.
- Have you ever spent time daydreaming and, if so, what about?

This is not an exhaustive list, but it will give you some insights in the way team members think. If the team has already been selected or formed, as a coach you to a certain extent have opened the doors for a coaching process by asking these questions. Furthermore, I will give some insights into the team dynamic before the work starts. If things go awry, you have a greater chance of improving things.

Team coaching process and critical success factors

I will discuss this section from an external coach consultant perspective, as that is my experience. The numbers of internal coaches are increasing these days, which means that large companies see the value of coaching. Where internal coaches do exist, they can be supplemented by specialist external coaches or ones who are specifically set aside for senior and executive leadership. Virtually all change management or transformation programmes involve consulting in addition to coaching, supported by thought leadership and a vision. In my experience, most large corporations do not carry as many internal consultants as they used to, so this element is supplemented from outside the organisation, usually led by either some internal thought leaders or key influencers.

If we refer to Figure 9.3, generally, we will be coaching on one topic at a time as needs must, and this will usually be post-workshop on a specific topic that has been identified as part of the project plan. Most of the transformations I have been involved with, both operating and consulting, comprise some level of upfront training or upskilling. As these transformations have been in the manufacturing arena and chemicals sector, the elements generally fall into specific categories, all of which have specific outcomes. There will also be one-to-one interventions required as part of a team coaching process, particularly if a member is struggling. These of course need to be treated in confidence in the same way as a normal one-to-one session.

Having spoken to other associates, who have delivered marketing and innovation-based cultural transformation, they have followed similar structured approaches. As with operational transformation, the initial focus has been on the clarity of the business outcome. In fact, where the transformations have struggled this was because the leadership strategy around marketing and innovation was unclear. To quote Mark Blackwell of Arkaro Consulting, quite often 'The leaders don't have an understanding of where to win and how to play.' Furthermore, those marketeers who are responsible for delivery end up with skills that they cannot use, because the leadership strategy is not clear. From a change management model perspective, this is a clear situation where you begin with the end in mind.

Figure 9.4 highlights some of the typical work elements that can lead to workshops that large companies or corporates should be working on or working towards, in support of fundamental programmes within the manufacturing and industrial sector, relating to manufacturing and operational performance, effective use of

Figure 9.4 Change management programmes model

capital and both process and behavioural safety. Most companies have some version of these programmes already but will require external consultancies and/or training organisations to rebuild, develop or reinvigorate them. These functional elements are all underpinned by coaching and the need for behavioural shift. Although there will be a level of knowledge transfer based on subject matter, the purpose of the workshop is to turn training and knowledge into action. The coaching process will support the knowledge transfer process. In my experience, the initial understanding of the concepts is easier than turning this knowledge into action. The action can present barriers in numerous ways. These can manifest as a lack of belief in the new methodologies, a fear of change, and concern about the volume of work, all of which may require coaching to varying degrees. In team coaching we are looking for real-time shifts in both behaviour and working patterns as a means of achieving the most powerful outcomes.

The coaching process

When we are coaching teams, they are still doing tangible work. Some of them will be taken out of their normal roles, and some will be taking part alongside their other work. The core purpose of coaching in this environment is to support the need for change. This is done by raising awareness and improving capabilities. The core outcome is to improve overall team performance, while working towards a common goal, collaboratively. An additional and important side benefit is generating a passion for the new approaches. The coach needs to be inspiring and energetic, and to support the change process. As I have mentioned before, co-creating the space and building trust are always the precursor. In coaching, we call this the 'contracting phase'. There are elements that support the trust-building before the tangible work happens on the team goal. If it is a new team, I always spend 30–45 minutes talking about the importance of acting like change agents, being self-aware, being non-judgemental, keeping a sense of perspective and self-regulating. Ask yourself the question, how many meetings or training sessions have you been to where the trainer starts off with stating the ground rules like this: 'Today's ground rules are, no phone interruptions, turn off PC, respect others' opinions', and many others? Unfortunately, trainees have become blind to these because they are delivered rapidly and almost superficially. Therefore, the contracting phase is so important, and I promote a discussion on the topics in the form of the 'Why'. This helps embed the understanding and strengthens the internal relationships. For those who are familiar with the 'forming, storming, norming and performing' model, this can be considered the forming stage, leading on to storming and norming. If the coaching of this specific team is going to last for months, then I will run a separate session. The trick for the coach is to remember that it is coaching, not training or even facilitation. Georgina Woudstra in her team coaching training, stresses the point about the importance of holding the space for the team to develop, rather than falling into the facilitation trap.[6] In the same way that there is still some confusion between group and team coaching, there is also some confusion between the roles of team coach and facilitator. I always check in with myself at the start of any programme and get other coaches I am leading to do the same.

Some teams are formed to solve short discrete problems or design something, others for a wider topic. As an example, I will use an analogy. In the arena of a process safety transformation, I have experience in both operations and consulting. In operations I acted as the programme leader for two UK sites, and in consulting I have acted as workstream leader/coach. I will discuss the operational experience first where the two sites were both acquisitions with virtually no process safety at all. Process safety transformations can and will take between three to five years to get close to sustainability. They have another unique challenge in that there is no direct financial return. The aim is to avoid large-consequence events that can cause death, injury, damage to assets, negative environmental impact and/or reputational damage. Fundamentally, this is a risk avoidance scenario that does not sit on the balance sheet, usually taking a very significant human and resource effort. In some respects, this can be considered 'utility value',[7] but in the context of a corporation rather than an individual. In the case where I led the programme, there was a gargantuan effort in pulling the team together, because it is not a subject people outside the discipline of engineering want to get involved in. Furthermore, the site was a very lean organisation, light on resources. The programme was a corporate-mandated requirement which would be audited and assessed. I recall there was a great deal of reticence about joining the team for the reasons mentioned above. It would be an addition to the 'day job', as it was for me too. Getting the team motivated was understandably a challenge. We had staff who did not understand the meaning of PSM (Process Safety Management), so considerable motivational coaching and grounding had to be done. There was also a need to create psychological safety, as discussed earlier. The team members were in a different space and it was important for them to feel shielded as they asked exploratory questions, which may have left them feeling vulnerable. There was team coaching during workshops and individual coaching outside of the formal sessions. In all, there were 15 key themes and we struggled to get more than five members in the core team, meaning that some members had multiple accountabilities with increasing workloads. Clearly there were some headwinds, but we had the advantage of a clear goal and a level of 'trench spirit'. As time went on, the team did expand and we put in more structure and regularity.

So, if I look back, I will reflect on what went well and what did not go so well. Even with a level of challenge/adversity a team can perform well. I think because all the team had minimal expertise, but reasonable functional knowledge, that helped. There was a considerable amount of reading or background work to be done. The selection of the team had to be based on functioning skills, intellect and curiosity. There were pre-discussions about suitability and workload. Even with an injection of energy and passion, and a sense of urgency, things got off to a slow start. There was considerable facilitation in the meetings and one-to-one coaching. Even setting up a meeting schedule was a challenge and initially some members did not turn up. I had to use some 'stick' as well as a 'carrot' with the backing of the site leader to ensure attendance. I do not want to present a picture that these sessions are always easy, even with moderate planning and pre-work. The one-to-one sessions mainly reinforced the vision and gave encouragement as well as listening to individual concerns. There was an additional challenge in that, due to the complexity of the work required, which was technical, process-led, and demanded considerable pre-work, it was going to be difficult to demonstrate success quickly and keep the team motivated. All my experience as a coach and leader told me I needed 'quick wins' especially with a team who hadn't really chosen to do the work. One thing I had learned from all my lean training was that faced with large complex issues, it is best to break them down into manageable chunks and get some quick wins. However, gaining quick wins at the expense of long-term effectiveness is never good. I worked with the team to ascertain what work could be done without compromise. Due to the nature of the age of the site, its chemical processes, structures, layouts and history, not all the data was available. However, we could build a roadmap and timescale. That way, we could get some early traction. We were able to split the workload across the 15 elements into easy and hard, based on workload. We had a timeline and milestones for all the elements. Although we did get some traction, it was still difficult to assess where the team was against the endpoint. I decided to invite the head of process safety across to the site for a few days and see if he could do an informal progress assessment. Fortunately, he agreed and over a period of three days and some hard work, he was able to share a score of 44 per cent. The minimum score for a first round assessment was 75 per cent and we were only 18 months away from the formal assessment. However, the score was better than the team expected so that gave us some motivation. With the assessment came a gap analysis which was both qualitative and quantitative, which also gave the team some clarity on where to go next. Our work had been structured as well as it could be at the start, but was still a bit haphazard. The focus and discipline increased with time, especially as the team members got to know one another. The requirement for team coaching still existed and one-to-ones still took place until the time for the formal assessment. There was a flurry of activity just before the formal assessment. However, the minimum hurdle was achieved, which, in the context of where we started, was well received, as the team initially thought it would be virtually impossible. There was also considerable shared learning through the experience in terms of knowledge and process. This process generates accelerated learning and harnesses the collective potential of this diverse team.

Some brief reflections on this experience:

- Get the balance right between heart and head. I have mentioned this before, but it is imperative you build trust at the start. Even with the head driving the need for structure and process to get the job done, if I had not engaged well at the start, we would not have succeeded. I always lead on engagement before systems and processes these days. As an engineer, that can be difficult, which is why I always anchor before sessions and try to use Figure 4.7 (p. 49) as my reference.
- It takes time for people to adjust and as a coach/leader you must be patient, especially when people are outside their comfort zones. In this situation, the team members were faced with alien concepts and processes, and needed time to make connections between their own skills.

- My own self-awareness was critical during this journey as it would have been very easy to move away from leading, coaching and facilitating, and become more transactional. I also had some of the elements to deliver, as well as guide others. I did not get it right all the time. In coaching parlance, this also means we must be self-regulated.

- It took some time, but the team performance improved and became more cohesive, moving away from requiring direction, and gained a level of interdependence through collaboration. I mentioned that team members were selected based on functioning expertise and curiosity, what became clear was that the unconditional collaboration developed along the journey and egos were left at home. Patrick Lencioni also highlights the point in his book, that high-functioning teams are composed of people who will put the team goal ahead of their personal goals. This was also emphasised in Georgina Woudstra's course on the art of team coaching.

- In team coaching we are looking for changes in patterns of behaviour and outcomes. This is also based on a level of respect and collaboration. The best teams can set their team working processes requiring less facilitation. It can be as simple as the cadence of the sessions, as in this case. Where teams can do this, it helps with long-term sustainability. Collaboration helps build the internal relationships and vice versa.

- It was not always easy to be clear in my own head as to when I was facilitating the team and when I was coaching the team. Others will face similar situations. Team coaching is all about the 'here and now' not about the future. As with individual coaching, the team coach must be 'in the present' and elucidate presence. It is about holding the space, not facilitating the process. Another way of fully understanding whether you are truly in team coaching mode is to ensure that you are flowing your attention between, self, the other and the situation. Team coaching requires a level of mastery which can be gained through training, understanding the concepts and experiential learning.

As I conclude this chapter, I have been attending the ICF UK Chapter Conference (virtually). With more than 600 participants the technology did work, even without the opportunities to socialise face to face. The sessions were interactive, with chat rooms, and highly productive. The conference was spread over four and a half days, giving the opportunity for all the sessions to be attended rather than a selection. Coaches could embrace technology and, in some cases, help with the design of AI bots.

Key takeaways

- Whether you are coaching teams or individuals, the first step in the process is to build trust. In the case of an individual, a short 'get to know you' session can be powerful. For a team, it will take time, and this is where an icebreaker moment can add value. If possible, get to know your team in advance.

- Having reflected on my own coaching experiences, researched other literature and authors, the attributions for group coaching and team coaching are still in the process of definition and development. This should not present a problem, but any coach or potential coach should do their research in addition to any training as this will give perspective.
- Keeping teams energised and motivated through protracted periods is not easy, especially where it is difficult to envision either the end point or sustainability. This is particularly difficult where the end point does not have a direct link to a financial return, as in process safety management.
- It is important not to underestimate the power of shared learning in the team environment.
- Another way to look at forming, storming, norming and performing is contracting leading to connection, leading to creativity in the coaching environment.
- The ICF core coaching competencies are a great reference point for those about to embark on a transformation programme. If these are followed religiously, then potential ethical or conflict issues should not arise.
- Virtual means of coaching for individuals and teams are becoming more prevalent. This presents some challenges but as coaches adapt their mindsets to using them, they will become more established.
- Team coaching is not the same as team facilitation and is about co-creating the space for teams to flourish. Team coaching only requires the appropriate level of intervention.
- Team coaching is in the ascendancy and will become more prevalent over time as companies see its true value. The ICF is developing some team coaching core competencies with the support of Georgina Woudstra and her team.
- Both team and individual coaching require personal mastery. The coach's in-built curiosity will help this journey.

The above reflections on my own experience dovetail quite nicely with the purposeful guide *High Performance Team Coaching*, by Doctors Peters and Carr,[8] who explain a structured approach to team coaching in their six-step model based on extensive literature surveys and collective experience. One of the points they do highlight is that it is not always possible to follow all the steps in the model for practical reasons. I know from my own experience that clients do not always afford you the time to follow all the elements of the model. Sharon Toye and Colin Price put a strong business case for team coaching in their book, *Accelerating Performance*.[9] They describe their META framework, standing for *Mobilise, Execute, Transform, Agility* as a means of driving team performance supported by coaching. As we move into even more competitive business environments with the advent of Big Data and digital, agility will be one of the key levers.

10 Embedding coaching for impact: How does the transformation stick?

Continuously developing culture

In this chapter I will attempt to cover some of the thinking and practical considerations for embedding a coaching culture within an organisation, not for its own sake but with success in mind. For any transformation to succeed and to be truly sustainable, the culture must be one that is curious, continually evolving and not afraid of change. A sustainable transformation is one where there is no 'hard stop'. It is where individuals and teams carry on using their newfound skills and processes. The new rituals are followed implicitly rather than leaders having to be explicit. These rituals are driven by intrinsic motivation rather than the need for compliance. If we use an example from manufacturing, this is where the line operator knows there is a problem and shuts down the line or slows it down instinctively, rather than passing it down the line and causing bigger problems later on. This is not about complacency. Accomplished leaders follow the principles previously laid out by quality gurus, that staff who find problems and raise them rather than staying quiet or acquiescing are the true heroes.

One of the overriding elements to embedding a coaching culture is to ensure that the workspace is conducive to coaching. This means it is a safe space where staff can experiment, challenge or debate without fear of any redress for this process. This is not about allowing people to drive actions without consequences or accountability.

The culture of constant checks and balances is the one that needs to be driven by leaders' understanding that is fair and appropriate. Leaders must role-model the correct behaviours. However, leaders have an extra responsibility. In this sense, I do not mean leaders who have line authority, I also mean the informal leaders who are both accountable and responsible for change. One of the perennial questions I have asked over the years when running behavioural safety workshops is, 'Who is responsible for safety on site or in the company?' Nine times out of ten, I get the textbook answer which is 'Everyone'. This is true, however there is also a subtle nuance which I always mention. I guide the participants that leaders have an extra accountability in that they have access to materials and resources. The danger of not doing this is that leaders in certain company cultures can effectively pass the buck down the line. This is a moot point about accountability and one of the reasons I stress this repeatedly in all my engagements. The 'passing the buck' phenomenon in part was one of the reasons for the inception of the crime of 'corporate manslaughter' in the UK in 2008 because the leadership teams were trying to collectively dilute responsibility after a fatality or serious event, so that no individual could be held accountable. Accountability is not something that can or should be diluted. Furthermore, I also remind leaders about the difference between delegation and either abdication or abrogation. This is something that is easily forgotten. I cannot stress it enough at the start of any engagement, as this is what sets the correct tone. I actively guide leaders to make their positions clear to their reports and emphasise that they must role-model the correct behaviour.

Sustainable mindset

I have stated this before but having a sustainable mindset is critical for embedding a coaching culture. 'Sustainability' is a word that can be over-used. What does it mean in this context? A sustainable mindset means that you truly believe in continuous improvement, and at the end of the transformation you will do everything in your power to ensure the staff also think this way. At the official end of any transformation it is critical to set up workshops and processes that will support continuous improvement and the need for coaching. This is also where coaching should have had an additional impact throughout the deployment, as coaches and coach leaders will have been reiterating the need for sustainability. There is always a conundrum in that having an official end point could, in theory, in some people's minds mean that the job is done. I learned early on to use the term key milestone rather than project close. If you take software development as an example, there is a constant process of evolution, even if there are some revolutions on the way. For these companies, the 'soft stop' may be the formal release of a new version. For the operational excellence transformations I have been involved with, we ran sustainability workshops, and reviewed KPIs to ensure sustainability was possible and achievable, and was set up in such a way that traction is maintained. There is a mutual symbiosis here where the process of coaching supports sustainability and vice versa. The former supports by helping the levels of focus and engagement with the staff, and the latter creates an understanding that a sustainable mindset requires regular coaching.

Figure 10.1 (p. 122) shows a typical continuous improvement organisation structure. This is a manufacturing example, but the principles apply to any type of organisation. The key principle is that you maintain an idea generation process, and these ideas should come from those closest to the challenges, i.e. shop floor workers and supervisors. You will need an idea review and validation process, which could be something you have designed with appropriate input from continuous improvement specialists and leaders, or maybe it is something you have available corporately. The best continuous improvement organisational structures I have seen also have senior continuous improvement sponsors working alongside the programme leaders as a way of showing leadership and accountability. As Figure 10.1 shows, these people

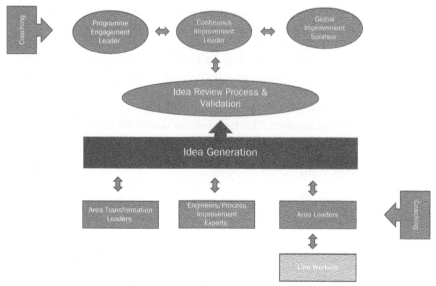

Figure 10.1 Change sustainability structure

may require coaching, but it is more likely to be individual and ad hoc. At the line level there could be some team coaching or ad hoc. The aim is to keep the energy levels up, and ideas flowing. In Chapter 5, I mentioned the use of sustainability trackers. This can be in the form of a simple dashboard or spreadsheet. It can include measures such as status of initiatives, specific business measures, engagement levels and many more. The key thing is to keep it visual and simple.

A final reflection on a sustainability mindset. Those who genuinely believe in sustainability are more likely to embrace coaching. They will know that they do not have all the answers and will seek help when needed.

Linking waste and productivity to a coaching mindset

I have discussed productivity throughout the book. That is because I believe it has a link with a coaching ethos, and have seen this on numerous occasions throughout my operational and consulting career. The word productivity has been part of our lexicon for years now. Productivity comes in many forms, manufacturing, digital, personal and team. In the context of culture shift and change, productivity goes beyond simple ratios, performance measures of output vs. input. Productivity is inexorably linked to having the correct mindset. In Japanese, the word for waste is 'muda'. The Japanese manufacturing culture has been constantly and consistently seeking out waste for 40+ years. It was originally defined as the seven wastes or, in some companies, the eight wastes (Figure 10.2). At its inception, the quality and manufacturing gurus got staff to think about waste in their organisation at all levels. There are very simple definitions that align with principles as a means of getting

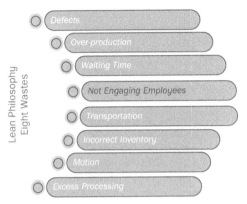

Figure 10.2 The eight wastes model

staff engagement and good levels of understanding. Originally pioneered by Toyota, other Japanese manufacturing companies, which are now global giants, followed suit. A great reference for how the Toyota company spread its influence around the world and helped others with its mantra is 'The Toyota Way'. This also covers other key aspects on training, coaching and the importance of continuous improvement cultures.[1] Toyota built a lot of its thinking around waste removal as 'muda' was the enemy of efficiency and effectiveness. The aim was to get all employees, no matter what level, to seek waste in the organisation. Initially it does not matter about the financial savings associated with it. It is all about the mindset. The thinking was simple: waste costs money, time and unnecessary effort. Once you have all the staff in this mindset, then the bandwidth for increasing productivity grows to the size of the total organisation. In DuPont we used the eight wastes model with a simple mnemonic, 'DOWNTIME' (as illustrated in Figure 10.2). The word itself has resonance as it implies that we should avoid unnecessary downtime to stay waste-free and productive.

Although the model originated in the automotive sector, it is easily translatable to all types of business, from any form of manufacturing to marketing, digital services, professional services, and other areas. I have lectured and delivered webinars on the potential of this approach to banks and the Institute of Directors. I have even guided internal consultants on how to use this model as a means of shifting data services from the web to the cloud. Its beauty is its simplicity and the principles hold good. This became the overarching model and approach for doing the transfer.

This approach drives curiosity, energy and focus. Strong productivity allows people to have a sense of achievement through performance. During our operational excellence transformation, we trained a large cohort of coaches globally. The criteria for selection of coaches were more to do with soft skills, such as emotional intelligence, energy and curiosity, more than functional and intellectual skills. The cohort we trained was probably equivalent to 1–2 per cent of the global manufacturing workforce. That may seem a small number but there was a minimum of one highly trained Mindset and Behaviours coach at each site, who could lead workshops and engagement sessions. Other coaches were trained to a lower level to

1. Base your management decisions on long-term philosophy, even at the expense of short-term financial goals

2. Create continuous process flow to bring problems to the surface

3. Use pull systems to avoid overproduction

4. Level out the workload (*Heijunka*)

5. Build a culture of stopping to fix problems, to get quality right first time

6. Standardised work is the foundation for continuous improvement and employee empowerment

7. Use visual control so no problems are hidden

8. Use only reliable, thoroughly tested technology that serves your people and processes

9. Grow leaders who thoroughly understand the work, live the philosophy and teach it to others

10. Develop exceptional people and teams who follow your company's philosophy

11. Respect your extended network of partners and suppliers by challenging them and helping them improve

12. Go and see for yourself to thoroughly understand the situation (*Genchi Genbutsu*)

13. Make decisions slowly by consensus, thoroughly considering all options, implement rapidly

14. Become a learning organisation through relentless reflection (*Hansei*) and continuous improvement (*Kaizen*)

Figure 10.3 Toyota's 14 principles

bandwidth and work with change agents. If we look back at Figure 10.1, the Site Improvement Champions were all sent on a two-week training course so they could aid implementation. This was a powerful experience as it was not just an effective learning opportunity, but gave them a great chance to network with other site leaders and discuss common challenges. I enjoyed the opportunity to understand other cultures from around the globe. This whetted my appetite for understanding differing regional cultures. Everything we learned was regarding performance, productivity and engagement. This is where I learned along with others that lean thinking and waste removal are dovetailed with coaching.

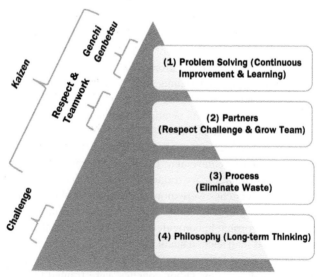

Figure 10.4 The 4P pyramid model, the Toyota Way

As part of Toyota's overarching philosophy, it developed its 14 principles, illustrated in Figure 10.3. If we look at the key facets of effective coaching such as curiosity, unearthing problems, culture, long-term thinking, developing people, respect for others, gaining consensus and fostering a learning organisation, the links between coaching and Toyota's principles are clear.

Another way of illustrating this is in the 4P pyramid, as shown in Figure 10.4. The base of the pyramid is the foundation stone or the philosophy of a learning organisation. If we look at level 3 and the levels above it, this is about process improvement and specifically removing waste. It is clear to see that coaching and the principles of lean are interwoven.

One of the reasons as both a productivity consultant and professional coach I am so passionate about waste removal is that passion drives the correct mindset and is consistent with being a powerful coach. Even within non-productivity-based cultural transformations, I always share the links as this builds the correct mindset and makes understanding easier.

Support networks

In my view, support networks are not as prevalent in the corporate world as they should be. Coaches and change agents need a support network for psychological safety, especially as they are going to push boundaries and there may be some kickback.

One of the ways in which companies and corporations can support coaches is by providing mentor coaches across the cohort. This is advocated by the ICF and forms part of its training and accreditation. Not only do mentor coaches provide support, they can also offer new ideas and thinking.

In addition to having mentor coaches, the ICF runs a series of formalised peer coaching cohorts, which I have found useful. Once you have signed up, you get to coach a peer and get coached by another. I find this system powerful as it allows you to choose your coach, based on skillset. I have completed three of these rounds now, and always ask for a professional who has a different niche talent and was trained at a different school. In that way I learn more and increase my personal bandwidth. This is particularly powerful if you are involved in a transformation, as you have someone to refer to outside the environment you are working in, which will provide a different perspective.

In addition to the ICF support and peer coaching networks, I have remained in close contact with all the coaches who were in my iPEC diploma cohort, to whom I can reach out when I need. As I have mentioned before, professional coaches have similar values, even with different approaches, which also helps. As I write this chapter, we are in the middle of a global crises, which outside any formal transformations, demonstrates the need for a support network, whether it be coaches or others.

Getting the mood right: compassion and gravitas

The heading of this section might seem a bit odd in the context of embedding a coaching culture. I referred to the concept in Chapter 6 as one of the concepts a coach can use when the circumstances are particularly harsh. I have labelled it a concept because it is not really an approach, but is more akin to a state of being. Even though it is quite subtle, it does have power in the coaching environment. As coaches, we are taught the concept of detached involvement. This is where we are guided to listen intently so we can coach effectively but ensure that we do not get over-involved. However, it is all right to show compassion where appropriate. I can recall showing it myself on a few occasions. It is fine to show compassion, but not necessarily be 'their friend'. This follows the principles of detached involvement.

Alongside compassion goes the need for gravitas in certain circumstances. One of the traps for coaches is that their desire to be understanding and empathetic may make them come across as potentially insincere or flippant, if the body language is empathetic. The probability is low, meaning that signals could be misread. I find it is possible to be understanding and show gravitas if the situation demands it. Showing gravitas can be very powerful as it demonstrates sincerity and embodies the 'whole coach'.

Creating a culture of effective challenge

Effective coaches challenge everything appropriately. An organisation that allows its staff, leaders and coaches to challenge will be considered a learning organisation. Without challenge an organisation will acquiesce to unnecessary conformity. Conformity is OK if it has a purpose in that it aids rigour or appropriate standardisation. Learning organisations are those that are creative and are continually evolving to meet the changing demands of business and the marketplace. At the start of the book, we discussed the importance of understanding the VUCA world. This is more prevalent than ever, with the rate of change decreasing from years to weeks in certain circumstances. The discussion is raging on business social media and in conferences about the need for challenge and creativity to balance the VUCA environment. Previous linear thinking will no longer be effective. Authors like Charles Duhigg and Peter Senge had given concrete examples of the importance of learning organisations even before the current complexity and volatility of the business environment.

How can effective coaching support the learning organisation? A coaching programme and framework can help to remove stagnation. Professional coaches will have been trained in how to help staff push their personal boundaries. This is a key part of any coaching culture. This is not about getting an organisation to push itself to a point where it stresses itself. It is about creative challenge that moves away from the status quo, and constructive tension in key meetings. Getting staff to surface issues rather than bury them. Therefore, having team facilitators in key meetings can be very powerful. In the numerous transformations I have been involved in, we have had a cohort of facilitators specifically designed to challenged. In the VA (Value Accelerator) programme we ran at DuPont, it was a two-day programme with testing and validation to become a facilitator. In a 2018 engagement where I was leading and coaching, I was relentless in my challenge of my function and other functions where appropriate. It was critical to get the team thinking differently as they had been stagnating for years. Peter Senge, in his book *The Fifth Discipline*, talks about one of the elements of historical stagnation with respect to 'Today's problems come from yesterday's solutions', in that if we are not thinking systemically, we are not challenging appropriately.[2]

One of the expressions that I use regularly with my clients is that they need to 'feel comfortable with being uncomfortable'. This is the new paradigm they will have to adopt. Transformations consume time, energy and resources, so the challenges must be appropriate to be embedded in the culture and not seen for challenge's sake. Once this culture becomes second nature as muscle memory, then future transformations will be easier.

Bring your team with you

This concept should be intuitive. A team is only as good as its weakest link. Any transformation programme is a marathon and not a sprint. My first exposure to this concept was a night exercise at a leadership training course back in the late 1980s during my time at BASF. Outdoor activities had become in vogue as vehicles for leadership training, along with team psychology. I remember clearly doing a team event in the Lake District using checkpoints and compasses. Prior to the event, one of the participants had already established himself as the 'alpha' in terms of physical fitness. He self-nominated to be the team leader, which was no great surprise. Fortunately for us, he was in one of the opposing teams. These events are never set up to test physical fitness but more geared towards teamwork, critical thinking and basic intelligence. I recall there were four or five teams. Two of the teams, including mine and the one led by the 'alpha', had members who had some level of physical difficulty. I remember our team took regular breaks on the way up the hills, allowing the slower members to catch up and even going back to them when they were struggling. We made it to the end successfully and we were not last. When we reached the end point, the 'alpha' leader had already arrived, but his team had not. The outcome was expected, he had left his team behind and his team came last, because the brief had been clear: the finish was effective only when the whole team crosses the line.

This was a very early and tangible lesson in the power of a team for me. I have carried this through my whole career from building new engineering and maintenance teams, large construction projects, operational excellence transformations and consulting engagements of varying sizes and complexities.

What does this mean for coaching teams that will be embedded in transformations? It will mean, as the lead coach, you will need to ensure that you do not leave your coaching team behind. This means that not only do you keep them up to speed on all the strategic developments, but you create your own learning organisation. It is critical that you create and reinforce the sense of curiosity within the team and ensure they feel safe to explore. It is important that the coach leader does not fall into the trap of being the total focal point. It is an opportunity to rotate roles and bring people on.

Dealing with the biases

This section of the chapter is intended to provoke thought and trigger internal or self-debate, and reveal one of the possible ways in which you can help embed a coaching culture. I stress the word 'help' here because I believe that ditching biases is an enabler for better coaching. In this context I am talking about cognitive biases. In Chapter 6, I talked about some of the cognitive biases highlighted by Daniel Kahneman. He also describes the two brain states, which are the intuitive brain and the logical and processing brain. In his book *Thinking, Fast and Slow*, he describes some of the illusions as well as factors that influence our intuition.[3] The reason I mention this is because, as coaches, as well as the power of active listening, we are told in certain cases to follow our intuition. Even in the world of probability and statistics we have 'Bayes' Theorem', which describes the probability of an event, based on prior knowledge of conditions that might be related to the event.[4] In psychology, this is sometimes seen as having a level of intuition as it has a link to prior knowledge.

In any coaching culture or programme the team needs to understand that cognitive and unconscious bias exists. Coaches must also follow their own intuition where appropriate. I am not going to explore every bias here and will leave it to the reader to do their own research, which will be enlightening. Coaches must be tuned, using their own self-awareness and presence, to recognise bias and take an appropriate course of action. Unconscious bias can come in many forms, whether it be gender, ethnicity, sexual orientation, age, class or cultural background, and, of course, neural approach. This must not just be considered part of the coaching process, but part of the preparation or contracting. Coaches are predominantly white and female and although there is a drive to change the diversity balance, we have a long way to go. Coaches must also be aware that certain genders and ethnicities are attracted to certain jobs and professions and actively shy away from others, and must foster a sense of inclusivity. The profession itself must embrace and encourage people from differing backgrounds to increase the bandwidth of the profession, ensuring less obvious work areas and levels are not left untouched. Junior levels must be considered, and the rise of reverse mentoring programmes will challenge the bias here.

A lead coach or programme leader should ensure that their coaches are aware of bias and through coaching experience learn in their own ways how to deal with it. This can be effected through workshops, awareness programmes, reading lists and experiential learning. Most of my associates and progressive heads of learning and development functions follow these practices. As coaching becomes more established and the number of internal coaches grows proportionately, then these practices will increase. The world is way more aware of unconscious bias than it was five years ago, through diversity programmes and other initiatives.

A couple of final reflections for this section. Dealing with bias is aligned with the ICF core competency around non-judgement. Getting coaches to go through supervision or having a coach mentor is powerful. Dealing with bias is not easy, and different coaches will handle it in different ways and at a different pace. The aim is not to eradicate it totally, just be aware that it exists at a personal level and in others. If there are open discussions about this within any coaching team or function, then the collective awareness will increase. These discussions should happen outside the function and that will also help embed a coaching culture.

Key takeaways

- Even if the core change objective is not productivity, then having a productive culture will support the sustainable mindset. Furthermore, those who are genuinely productive are more likely to embrace coaching, i.e. be coached and give coaching.
- Developing a continuous improvement structure aids both a learning organisation and the philosophy of coaching.
- Having an independent support network for coaches supports the need for psychological safety and aids new thinking along with coach personal development.
- If a company truly wants to embed coaching in its organisation, then it needs to let coaches be relatively free in terms of thought, creativity and approach. It is OK to have a framework, but too much constraint will stifle progress. As I have mentioned before, coaches are a different breed and will need their own psychological safety.
- Effective challenge is critical for having the correct organisational culture and vice versa. The point is to confront issues and not get into conflict with people. An effective challenge culture should become muscle memory.
- One other way we can embed a coaching culture is to build a roadmap for coaching at the start. The starting point will depend on where your coaching culture stands at the time. It would be quite easy to build a roadmap based on some of the elements mentioned in this chapter and others. Building a bespoke roadmap would be a powerful visualisation for generating and sustaining a coaching culture. I have started this with new clients.
- Unconscious bias exists everywhere and will never be eradicated. It is the way that coaches and leaders deal with it that matters.

11 Conclusion: Reflections and key takeaways

What is required for success?

I will pick out some key reflections that are not mentioned in the chapter summaries to allow the reader to start pulling their thoughts together in a way that provides some overall context to the coaching process with respect to change and transformation.

Coaching as a profession is still in its infancy, so it is still developing and forming, particularly in the arena of team coaching. This a huge opportunity for creation and application of new thinking. This will support the wider implementation of a coaching culture within organisations. As the market changes dramatically, organisations will have to respond to significant change. In this context the market means the job market, working culture, work–life balance and business dynamics, with VUCA at the forefront of leaders' minds.

A significant number of cultural transformations fail, which is why coaching is so important. It is too early to get macro data on the impact of coaching on change. However, my own experience from many deployments is clear. Those that do not have it, or have the coaching stop too early, have an increased risk of failure. There is a clear caveat in that the coaching programme must be structured and focused, i.e. not coaching for coaching's sake. As I mentioned earlier, it is not easy to directly link coaching to positive macro outcomes for the programmes, but shifts in behaviour can be monitored such as the effectiveness of meetings or specific initiatives. Companies will probably not want to run hypothesis tests on initiatives when they are running similar initiatives with and without coaching unless the risk of failure is small. The aim is to make a change.

- However, in the early 2000s, Manchester Inc. surveyed 100 executives, most of whom were from Fortune 1000 companies. The research showed that a company's investment in executive coaching realised an average ROI of almost six times the cost of the coaching.[1]
- The International Coaching Federation has highlighted that 86 per cent of organisations saw a ROI on their coaching engagements, and 96 per cent of those who had an executive coach said they would repeat the process.

These results are supported by tangible improvements, not just intangible ones, such as behavioural change. Typical results include improved sales as well as productivity and stakeholder engagement.

In certain quarters, coaching is still seen as 'quackery' or quasi science. That can be a blocker at an organisational level. At an individual level, the suggestion of coaching could imply a level of failure for some people. Therefore, it is important to demonstrate total transparency at the start. The objectives of the coaching programme and how it is linked to the desired transformation need to be clear and communicated. If the leadership plans to use a recognised change model, that should be explained and where coaching will have an impact should be highlighted. The purpose and ethics, including confidentiality, must be clearly stated.

The leadership team need to be determined, with patience and resolve. They must be transparent when things go wrong and demonstrate the appropriate level of vulnerability. The power of vulnerability is coming to the fore now, and exercising confident humility as a leadership trait has benefit. The pandemic crisis at the time of writing has amplified this.

I have seen so many programmes fail due to initiative overload. Before embarking on any transformation programme, leaders must have a good appreciation of what else is going on in the organisation to ensure they have the resources and bandwidth to complete the work. Ensure that there enough coaches in place to drive and sustain the programme.

As part of coach training, coaches are taught to deal with their own barriers and energy blockers. In certain cases, these can be fears related to their own impact and performance. One of the things that coaches and programme leaders can do is to formally recognise this, so that the coaches can feel a level of psychological safety. This will give them room to explore and be more effective. An organisation will recognise this culture subliminally and that will help the embedding process.

Finally, any programme needs an excellent and engaged leader. Leadership qualities are well defined these days, but one I think that is not recognised enough is that of clear and concise language, i.e. do not bamboozle. Unfortunately, we live in a world of acronyms and buzz words, which serve no purpose apart from potentially showing passive aggression. The over-use of these wastes time and causes confusion. Great leaders and coaches also know when to have the right perspective. They can have a strategic view in the 'helicopter' or a tactical view in the 'weeds'. Both are required; the trick is to know when and where to be, which is what I referred to in Chapter 4.

I recently read a great quotation from Liverpool football player Virgil Van Dijk, 'I just like playing for Liverpool, it really does not matter who is standing next to me.' The cultural transformation around passion and inclusivity at Liverpool under the guidance of Jürgen Klopp is considered one of the greatest of any recent leader. This quotation highlights to me that if you have a great culture everyone will want to be part of it and you will have a great performance. From a coach perspective, they will be used to working with anyone.

12   Future opportunities: Cultural transformation is a continuous journey

The coaching community is expanding as more people become professionally trained. Coaching is clearly a demand-led fraternity. Significantly more internal coaches are being hired within organisations as it is recognised that coaching offers a huge opportunity for impact. External coaches should embrace this rather than fear it. A significant number of external coaches will have left the corporate world and will be enjoying their freedom and expanded space. They may fear the prospect of going back to a large corporation. One of the coaching mantras is the concept of 'abundance' which means there is enough work for everyone. The feeling from the recent ICF UK conference was that the number of internal coaches will grow. In the same way that engineering and marketing functions use outsourced resources, then external coaches could still support internal coaches.

Agile thinking has been around in manufacturing and IT for more than 10 years. This same thinking will help cultural programmes and change management for businesses that are dealing with the VUCA environment. Agile is about not over-designing or coming to conclusions too early and going off track. It is about working in parallel, coming to a key milestone and reviewing. What does 'agile' mean for coaching in the context of change management? When dealing with individual clients, coaches must be agile in terms of active listening and thinking on their feet. They also must recognise when things are not working well and be prepared to adapt. Within the context of team coaching the coaches will need to get guidance and alignment with programme leaders around key milestones for each team or sub-team. Each team will have to collaborate more than before to ensure the requirements of the roadmap are made. Agile is a state of mind, like lean, not just an approach or a series of tools. Getting the agile mindset embedded in the organisation will have a positive impact. Effectiveness will come out of agility. The agility will also aid a continuous learning process, which I have mentioned before.

My belief is that we will see a considerable increase in coach training on the management agenda. With the rise in demand for internal coaches, we will see an expectation that senior leaders will be formally trained in coaching. The coaching schools and universities are open for business. The attributes of coaches are what are required for senior leaders and the training will expand their minds, reinforce

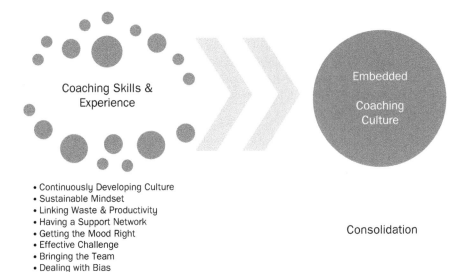

Coaching Skills & Experience

- Continuously Developing Culture
- Sustainable Mindset
- Linking Waste & Productivity
- Having a Support Network
- Getting the Mood Right
- Effective Challenge
- Bringing the Team
- Dealing with Bias

Embedded

Coaching Culture

Consolidation

Figure 12.1   The coalescence model

positive behaviours and emphasise understanding the critical ethics that are required for a coach. The more leaders can role-model the correct approaches, the better leaders they will become. Coaching will play a greater role and will have to be evidence-based, i.e. data or information will have to sit behind the thinking. As more organisations engage with coaching, this will help this process. As opposed to trade organisations, coaching fraternities are not afraid to share information and actively seek out sharing opportunities. Figure 12.1 shows the future of coaching: all the coaching skills and experience will become embedded in the coaching culture and will be consolidated.

One of the main challenges for coaching now is diversity. As it stands, the profession is, as mentioned earlier, predominantly composed of coaches who are white and female. As the world gradually becomes more attuned to neurodiversity, it is to be hoped that the balance will shift. Male professional coaches need to come forward and recognise their own emotional intelligence.

Technology will play an increasing role in coaching and this will go beyond video workshops and coaching sessions. Firms are also experimenting with interactive video with embedded Q&A at critical decision points. It is possible to do remote coaching based on differing scenarios and outcomes. A typical topic could be 'having a difficult conversation'. Although transactional in nature, these can be followed up with either face-to-face or video coaching. Some coaches are already using virtual reality (VR) for sessions and researching the effectiveness of using headsets. The key point is that the proportion of face-to-face coaching will decrease. It will probably decrease but never totally disappear. However, AI (artificial intelligence) coaching bots are being worked on right now. The early data is good, with respondents reporting feeling that issues were being dealt with and the session flowed well.

Given that coaching is all about the client in a coaching relationship and responding to the situation, this has greater potential than people imagine. As the AI develops, the emotional intelligence element will increase, improving the coaching experience.

One final thought on coaching for transformation: every coach needs to be prepared to do the appropriate level of research into the transformation journey and the requirements. This will become more important as time goes on. The days of 'arrive and drive' are over.

Notes

Chapter 1

1. Work done by Katharine Cook Briggs and her daughter Isabel Briggs Myers, with their Myers–Briggs Type Indicator (MBTI) personality profiling tool. My most recent result in 2018 was ENTP.
2. The concepts of Time vs. Through Time originate in Timeline Therapy, where Through Time is considered a generalised overview from a slightly dissociated perspective.
3. Carolyn Gregoire, 'How left-handed people think and feel differently: being a leftie is far from a disadvantage', Huffington Post, 1 December 2016.
4. Kotter's 8-step change model is found in J.P. Kotter, *Leading Change* (Boston: Harvard Business School Press, 1996).
5. J.L. Bennet and M.W. Bush, *Coaching for Change* (London: Routledge, 2013).
6. A coach leader is someone who is considered a leader and has the skills of a coach.
7. With the rise of such companies as Amazon and Google, creative companies are now selling their own form of product.

Chapter 2

1. T. Crabb, national director, research, at Cushman & Wakefield, 'The pace of technological change', *Australian Property Journal*, 18 October 2018. Available at: https://www.australianpropertyjournal.com.au/2018/10/18/the-pace-of-technological-change/
2. C. Maheshkar and V. Sharma, *Handbook of Research on Cross-Cultural Business Education* (Hershey, PA: IGI Global, 2018).
3. Geert Hofstede is an eminent psychologist, well known for his work on interculturality.
4. 'Culture', *Oxford English Dictionary*.
5. M. Barrier, 'Building a healthy company culture', *Nation's Business*, September 1997. Available at: https://www.inc.com/encyclopedia/corporate-culture.html
6. C. Coffman and K. Sorenson, *Culture Eats Strategy for Lunch* (Denver, CO: Liang Addison Press, 2013).
7. The iceberg model of culture was developed by noted anthropologist Edward T. Hall to help explain the breadth of culture (e.g. Hall, 1989).
8. Paul Terry, Sean Gill and C. Brooklyn Derr, 'Career orientations: multi-generational talent management'. Available at: www.kornferry.com/content/dam/kornferry/docs/

9. First introduced in the 1950s, RACI was originally called the 'Decision Rights Matrix' and is also known as 'Responsibility Charting'.
10. See Geert Hofstede's six dimensions of interculturality. Available at: https://hi.hofstede-insights.com/national-culture
11. Peter Salovey and John D. Mayer coined the term 'Emotional Intelligence' in 1990, describing it as 'a form of social intelligence that involves the ability to monitor one's own and others' feelings and emotions, to discriminate among them, and to use this information to guide one's thinking and action'.
12. Marshall C. Goldsmith, *What Got You Here Won't Get You There: How Successful People Become Even More Successful* (London: Profile Books, 2008).
13. P. Laurence and R. Hull, *The Peter Principle: Why Things Always Go Wrong* (New York: Harper Business, 2011).
14. Mark Buchanan, 'Why we are all creatures of habit', *New Scientist*, 4 July 2007.
15. M. Beer and N. Nohria, 'Cracking the code of change', in *HBR's 10 Must Reads on Change Management* (Boston: Harvard Business Review Press, 2011).
16. Inner work is the psychological and spiritual practice of diving deep into your inner self for the purposes of self-exploration, self-understanding and healing. Put simply, the internal thought processes we need to have to improve our personal performance.
17. Paul Hunter, *The Seven Inconvenient Truths of Business Strategy* (London: Routledge, 2016).

Chapter 3

1. Attributed to footballer Peter Shilton, the England goalkeeper.
2. J. Cockburn-Evans, Enable & Accelerate®.
3. Takt is the customer demand or purchase rate. When used as in Takt time, it means the interval between purchase, or call-off.
4. M.C. Goldsmith, *What Got You Here Won't Get You There: How Successful People Become Even More Successful* (London: Profile Books, 2008).
5. See Scott Adams' website at https://dilbert.com/strip/2014-03-26 for the relevant dates: 26 March 2014, 27 March 2014, 28 March 2014.
6. Neurodiversity is the range of differences in individual brain function and behavioural traits regarded as part of normal variation in the human population, used especially in the context of autism spectrum disorders.

Chapter 4

1. Paul Hunter, *The Seven Inconvenient Truths of Business Strategy* (London: Routledge, 2016).
2. 'Darwinism' is a term associated with Charles Darwin and his (1859) book, *On the Origin of Species*, referring to the need to adapt, and in a management context, the ability to adapt can be more significant than absolute strength.

3. Agile working is used in both project management and software development. It is a means of developing quickly against key milestones, avoiding wasted time associated with a totally linear approach.

4. P. Hemp and T.A. Stewart, 'Leading change when business is good: an interview with Samuel J. Palmisano', in HBR, *HBR's 10 Must Reads on Change Management* (Boston: Harvard Business Review Press, 2011).

5. See Geert Hofstede's six dimensions of intraculturality. Available at: https://hi.hofstede-insights.com/national-culture

6. Enable & Accelerate® is a registered trademark of John Cockburn-Evans.

7. The 60:40 rule has its origins in investment deals whereby you have 60 per cent in risk stocks and 40 per cent in lower-risk stocks to get the best returns.

8. I discovered Energy Blocker, a concept introduced as part of my coaching within iPEC, i.e. a mental block that can negatively impact your energy. Some say the concept of blocking energy goes back to the days of Aristotle, later considered by Julian Huxley, Freud and others.

9. D. Ravasi and M. Schultz, 'Responding to organizational identity threats: exploring the role of organizational culture', *Academy of Management Journal*, 49(3) (2006).

10. Deal and Kennedy (2000) defined organisational culture as the way things get done around here. They refer to Schein's model. Kotter also talks about subcultures in his numerous texts. Kotter's 8-step model will be covered in Chapter 5.

11. Boris Groysberg, Jeremiah Lee, Jesse Price and J. Yo-Jud Cheng, 'The leader's guide to corporate culture', *Harvard Business Review*, 1 January 2018.

12. Hunter, *Seven Inconvenient Truths*, op. cit.

13. W. Chan Kim and Renee Mauborgne, 'Tipping point leadership', *Harvard Business Review*, April 2003.

14. Richard Edelman is CEO and President of Edelman PR Company.

15. Scott Judd, Eric O'Rourke and Adam Grant, 'Employee surveys are still one of the best ways to measure engagement', *Harvard Business Review*, 14 March 2018.

16. P. Morrel-Samuels, 'Getting the truth into workplace surveys', *Harvard Business Review*, February 2002. Available at: https://hbr.org/2002/02/getting-the-truth-into-workplace-surveys

Chapter 5

1. Marshall C. Goldsmith, *What Got You Here Won't Get You There: How Successful People Become Even More Successful* (London: Profile Books, 2008).

2. Chirag Metre, 'Deriving value from change management', thesis, University of Pennsylvania, 2009. Available at: repository.upenn.edu/cgi/viewcontent.cgi?article=1027&

3. K. Lewin, 'Group decision and social change', in E.E. Maccoby, T.M. Newcomb and E.L. Hartley (eds), *Readings in Social Psychology* (New York: Holt, Rinehart and Winston, 1958), pp. 197–211.

4. Todd Jick, '10-stage change management model', in T. Jick and M. Peiperl, *Managing Change: Cases and Concepts* (New York: McGraw-Hill, 2003).

5.   John P. Kotter, *Leading Change* (Boston: Harvard Business School Press, 1996).
6.   PROSCI® and ADKAR® are licensed trademarks of the PROSCI Company.
7.   Richard Bandler and John Grinder are considered the founders of NLP.
8.   Marcus Buckingham, 'The fatal flaw with 360 surveys', *Harvard Business Review*, 17 October 2011.
9.   MBTI – the Myers–Briggs Type Indicator – describes 16 personality types relating to four focus areas, looking both outwards and inwards.
10. Laura Delizonna, 'High-performing teams need psychological safety: here's how to create it', *Harvard Business Review*, 24 August 2017.
11. Charles Duhigg, *The Power of Habit* (New York: Random House, 2013).
12. DocuSign® is a trademark of the Adobe Corporation.

Chapter 6

1.   S. Fry, J. Peterson, M.E. Dyson and M. Goldberg, *Political Correctness Gone Mad?* (London: Oneworld Publications, 2018).
2.   Maslow's hierarchy of needs is a famous theory in psychology proposed by Abraham Maslow in his 1943 article in *Psychological Review*, 'A theory of human motivation', 50(4): 370–96.
3.   Daniel Kahneman is an eminent psychologist who writes about cognitive bias. His book, *Thinking, Fast and Slow* (Harmondsworth: Penguin, 2012), is a classic.
4.   Philip Zimbardo, Craig Haney, W. Curtis Banks and David Jaffe, 'Stanford Prison Experiment 1971'. Available at: https://web.stanford.edu/dept/spec_coll/uarch/exhibits/Narration.pdf
5.   Passive-aggressive behaviour might include avoiding direct or clear communication, evading problems, fear of intimacy or competition, making excuses, blaming others, obstructionism, playing the victim, feigning compliance with requests, sarcasm, backhanded compliments and hiding anger.

Chapter 7

1.   Charles Duhigg, *The Power of Habit* (New York: Random House, 2013).
2.   Georgina Woudstra, Team Coaching Programme, 'The art of team coaching'. Available at: https://www.coaching-at-work.com/wp-content/uploads/2013/06/masterclass_flyer_georgina_woudstra_web.pdf

Chapter 8

1.   P.M. Lencioni, *The Five Dysfunctions of a Team: A Leadership Fable*, enhanced edition (Hoboken, NJ: John Wiley & Sons, 2010).
2.   Originally taken from 'The four stages of competence' by Martin M. Bradwell in 1969. See en.wikipedia.org/wiki/Four_stages_of_competence

3. Bruce Schneider, Energetic Self-Perception model, Institute for Professional Excellence in Coaching. Available at: https://www.energyleadership.com/assessment

4. Rich Fernandez, '5 ways to boost your resilience at work', *Harvard Business Review*, 6 June 2016.

5. Dr John Briffa, *A Great Day at the Office* (London: Fourth Estate, 2015).

6. Linda Graham, concepts taken from her books, *Resilience* (Novato, CA: New World Library, 2018) and *Bouncing Back* (Novato, CA: New World Library, 2013).

7. Greater Good Science Center, UC Berkeley, is a not for profit organisation focused on well-being.

8. Lencioni, *The Five Dysfunctions of a Team*, op. cit.

Chapter 9

1. Alexander Caillet, founder of Corentus and Mobius Executive Leadership, 'The team adaptability advantage', 2017.

2. Georgina Woudstra, 'Coaching individuals in a group context such as in action learning sets'. Available at: https://www.coaching-at-work.com/wp-content/uploads/2013/06/masterclass_flyer_georgina_woudstra_web.pdf

3. The GROW coaching model was originally developed by Sir John Whitmore in the 1980s and subsequently modified by others.

4. See J.R. Katzenbach and D.K. Smith's definition of a team in *The Wisdom of Teams* (New York: McGraw-Hill, 2015). There are many definitions, but this is widely considered one of the most relevant.

5. Martha E. Mangelsdorf's interview with Evan Apfelbaum, 'The trouble with homogeneous teams', *MIT Sloan Management Review*, 11 December 2017.

6. Georgina Woudstra, Team Coaching Programme, 'The art of team coaching'. Available at: https://www.coaching-at-work.com/wp-content/uploads/2013/06/masterclass_flyer_georgina_woudstra_web.pdf

7. Utility value is defined as the perceived importance of an activity because of its usefulness to other tasks or aspects of an individual's life (e.g. perceiving geometry to be valuable because it applies to engineering).

8. Dr Catherine Carr and Dr Jacqueline Peters, *High Performance Team Coaching* (Victoria, BC: Friesen Press, 2013).

9. Colin Price and Sharon Toye, *Accelerating Performance: How Organizations Can Mobilize, Execute, and Transform with Agility* (Hoboken, NJ: Wiley, 2017).

Chapter 10

1. The Toyota Company is considered the 'parent' of continuous improvement in the manufacturing sector.

2. Peter Senge, *The Fifth Discipline* (New York: Random House, 2006), originally published in 1990.

3. Daniel Kahneman, *Thinking, Fast and Slow* (Harmondsworth: Penguin, 2012).
4. Bayes' Theorem describes conditional probabilities. Its significance was first appreciated by the British cleric Thomas Bayes in his posthumously published masterpiece, 'An essay toward solving a problem in the doctrine of chances' (Bayes, 1764).

Chapter 11

1. Joy McGovern et al., 'Maximizing the impact of executive coaching', *The Manchester Review*, 6(1) (2001).

Bibliography

Bandler, R. and Grinder, J. (1990) *Frogs into Princes: Neuro Linguistic Programming*, Eden Grove Editions. Available at: https://openlibrary.org/publishers/Eden_Grove_Editions

Beer, M. and Nohria, N. (2011) 'Cracking the code of change', in HBR, *HBR's 10 Must Reads on Change Management*, Boston: Harvard Business Review Press.

Bennet, J.L. and Bush, M.W. (2013) *Coaching for Change*, London: Routledge.

Briffa, J. (2015) *A Great Day at the Office: 10 Simple Strategies for Maximising Your Energy and Getting the Best Out of Yourself and Your Day*, London: Fourth Estate.

Buchanan, M. (2007) 'Why we are all creatures of habit', *New Scientist*. Available at: https://www.newscientist.com/article/mg19526111-700-why-we-are-all-creatures-of-habit/

Buckingham, M. (2011) 'The fatal flaw with 360 surveys', *Harvard Business Review*, 17 October. Available at: https://hbr.org/2011/10/the-fatal-flaw-with-360-survey

Caillet, A. and Yeager, A. (2019) 'The team adaptability advantage: how flexible teams optimize effectiveness through multiple operating modes', Corentus. Available at: https://corentus.com/understanding-team-operating-modes#

Carr, C. and Peters, J. (2013) *High Performance Team Coaching*, Victoria, BC: Friesen Press.

Coffman, C. and Sorenson, K. (2013) *Culture Eats Strategy for Lunch: The Secret of Extraordinary Results*, Denver, CO: Liang Addison Press.

Delizonna, L. (2017) 'High-performing teams need psychological safety. Here's how to create it', *Harvard Business Review*, 24 August. Available at: https://hbr.org/2017/08/high-performing-teams-need-psychological-safety-heres-how-to-create-it

Duhigg, C. (2013) *The Power of Habit*, New York: Random House.

Duhigg, C. (2017) *Smarter, Faster, Better: The Transformative Power of Real Productivity*, New York: Doubleday.

Ellis, K. et al. (eds) (2018) *Interdisciplinary Approaches to Disability: Looking Forward to the Future*, vol. 2, New York: Routledge.

Fernandez, R. (2016) '5 ways to boost your resilience at work', *Harvard Business Review*, 6 June. Available at: www.hbr.org/2016/06/627-building-resilience-ic-5-ways-to-build-your-personal-resilience-at-work

Fry, S., Peterson, J., Dyson, M.E. and Goldberg, M. (2018) *Political Correctness Gone Mad?*, London: Oneworld Publications.

Goldsmith, M.C. (2008) *What Got You Here Won't Get You There: How Successful People Become Even More Successful*, London: Profile Books.

Graham, L. (2013) *Bouncing Back: Rewiring Your Brain for Maximum Resilience and Well-Being*, Novato, CA: New World Library.

Graham, L. (2018) *Resilience*, Novato, CA: New World Library.

Gregoire, C. (2016) 'How left-handed people think and feel differently: being a leftie is far from a disadvantage', *Huffington Post*, 1 December. Available at: https://www.huffingtonpost.co.uk/entry/left-handed-personality-psychology

Groysberg, B., Lee, J., Price, J. and Yo-Jud Cheng, J. (2018) 'The leader's guide to corporate culture', *Harvard Business Review*, 1 January.

Hall, E.T. (1989) *Beyond Culture*, New York: Anchor Books.

Hemp, P. and Stewart, T.A. (2011) 'Leading change when business is good: an interview with Samuel J. Palmisano', in HBR, *HBR's 10 Must Reads on Change Management*, Boston: Harvard Business Review Press.

Hunter, P. (2016) *The Seven Inconvenient Truths of Business Strategy*, London: Routledge.

James, T. (2017) *Time Line Therapy and the Basis of Personality*, Carmarthen: Crown House Publishing Ltd.

Jick, T. and Peiperl, M. (2003) *Managing Change: Cases and Concepts*, New York: McGraw-Hill.

Judd, S., O'Rourke, E. and Grant, A. (2018) 'Employee surveys are still one of the best ways to measure engagement', *Harvard Business Review*, 14 March. Available at: https://hbr.org/2018/03/employee-surveys-are-still-one-of-the-best-ways-to-measure-engagement

Jung, C.G. (2014) *Psychological Types*, London: Routledge.

Kahneman, D. (2012) *Thinking, Fast and Slow*, Harmondsworth: Penguin.

Kahneman, D. and Tversky, A. (2000) *Choices, Values, and Frames*, Cambridge: Cambridge University Press.

Katzenbach, J.R. and Smith, D.K. (2015) *The Wisdom of Teams: Creating the High-Performance Organization*, Boston: Harvard Business Review Press.

Kim, W.C. and Mauborgne, R. (2003) 'Tipping point leadership', *Harvard Business Review*, April. Available at: https://hbr.org/2003/04/tipping-point-leadership

Kotter, J.P. (1996) *Leading Change*, Boston: Harvard Business School Press.

Laurence, P. and Hull, R. (2011) *The Peter Principle: Why Things Always Go Wrong*, New York: Harper Business.

Lencioni, P.M. (2010) *The Five Dysfunctions of a Team: A Leadership Fable*, Hoboken, NJ: John Wiley & Sons, Inc.

Lewin, K. (1958) 'Group decision and social change', in E.E. Maccoby, T.M. Newcomb and E.L. Hartley (eds) *Readings in Social Psychology*, New York: Rinehart & Wilson, pp. 197–211.

Maheshkar, C. and Sharma, V. (2018) *Handbook of Research on Cross-Cultural Business Education*, Hershey, PA: IGI Global.

Mangelsdorf, M.E (2017) 'Evan Apfelbaum interview: the trouble with homogenous teams', *MIT Sloan Management Review*, 11 December. Available at: https://sloanreview.mit.edu/article/the-trouble-with-homogeneous-teams/

Maslow, A.H. (1943). 'A theory of human motivation', *Psychological Review*, 50(4): 370–96.

McGovern, J. et al. (2001) 'Maximizing the impact of executive coaching: behavioural change, organizational outcomes, and return on investment', *The Manchester Review*, 6(1).

Metre, C. (2009) 'Deriving value from change management', thesis, Master of Science in Organizational Dynamics, University of Pennsylvania. Available at: http://repository.upenn.edu/od_theses_msod/28

Morrel-Samuels, P. (2002) 'Getting the truth into workplace surveys', *Harvard Business Review*, February. Available at: https://hbr.org/2002/02/getting-the-truth-into-workplace-surveys

O'Malley, J. (2009) *Four Cultures of the West*, Boston: Harvard University Press.

Price, C. and Toye, S. (2017) *Accelerating Performance: How Organizations Can Mobilize, Execute, and Transform with Agility*, Hoboken, NJ: John Wiley & Sons, Inc.

Ravasi, D. and Schultz, M. (2006) 'Responding to organizational identity threats: exploring the role of organizational culture', *Academy of Management Journal*, 49(3).

Salovey, P. et al. (2004) *'Emotional Intelligence: Key Readings on the Mayer and Salovey Model*, New York: National Professional Resources, Inc.

Schein, E.H. (2016) *Organizational Culture and Leadership*, Hoboken, NJ: John Wiley and Sons, Inc.

Senge, P.M. (2006) *The Fifth Discipline*, New York: Random House Business.

Suri, R. (1998) *Quick Response Manufacturing: A Companywide Approach to Reducing Lead Times*, Boca Raton, FL: CRC Press.

Taff, A. (2018) *Bayes Theorem: The Ultimate Beginners Guide to Bayes' Theorem*, Createspace Independent Publishing Platform.

Terry, P., Gill, S. and Brooklyn Derr, C. (2008–11) 'Career orientations: multi-generational talent management', Global Novations. Available at: https://www.kornferry.com/content/dam/kornferry/docs/article-migration/CareerOrientations_MultigenTalentMgmt.pdf

Whitmore, J. (1996) *Coaching for Performance*, London: Nicholas Brealey Publishers.

Zimbardo, P., Haney, C., Banks, W.C. and Jaffe, D. (1971) 'The Stanford Prison Experiment', Stanford, CA. Available at: https://web.stanford.edu/dept/spec_coll/uarch/exhibits/Narration.pdf

Index